1000
D0446106

SIR GAWAIN
AND THE GREEN KNIGHT

A NEW VERSE TRANSLATION

W. W. NORTON & COMPANY, INC.
also publishes

THE NORTON ANTHOLOGY OF ENGLISH LITERATURE
edited by M. H. Abrams et al.

THE NORTON ANTHOLOGY OF POETRY
edited by Arthur M. Eastman et al.

WORLD MASTERPIECES
edited by Maynard Mack et al.

THE NORTON READER
edited by Arthur M. Eastman et al.

THE NORTON FACSIMILE OF
THE FIRST FOLIO OF SHAKESPEARE
prepared by Charlton Hinman
and the NORTON CRITICAL EDITIONS

SIR GAWAIN
AND THE GREEN KNIGHT

A NEW VERSE TRANSLATION

by

MARIE BORROFF

YALE UNIVERSITY

W · W · NORTON & COMPANY · INC · *New York*

COPYRIGHT © 1967 BY W. W. NORTON & COMPANY, INC.

Library of Congress Catalog Card No. 67-16601

All Rights Reserved

Published simultaneously in Canada by
George J. McLeod Limited, Toronto

ISBN 0 393 04220 0 Cloth Edition
ISBN 0 393 09754 4 Paper Edition

PRINTED IN THE UNITED STATES OF AMERICA

9 0

Contents

Introduction

Sir Gawain and the Green Knight, in its original Middle English form, is recognized as a literary work of the highest quality. Yet it has been known to us for only a hundred years, and it remains largely inaccessible to the nonspecialist because of the difficulty of its language, a language far more remote from the English of the present than that of Geoffrey Chaucer's London.

Gawain first turns up in modern history in a manuscript belonging to the library of the great antiquarian of Elizabethan times, Sir Robert Cotton. Cotton, in turn, seems to have obtained the manuscript from a library in Yorkshire; this is not surprising, for the *Gawain* poet must have lived somewhere in the Midlands of England, probably near present-day Stafford. He was a contemporary of Chaucer's, but there is little likelihood that Chaucer ever heard of him or knew his works.

The single manuscript in which *Gawain* is found contains three other poems generally considered to be the work of the *Gawain* poet. Two of these, called *Patience* and *Purity*, are written in the same alliterative verse-form as *Gawain*; the third, called *Pearl*, is in an elaborate rhymed stanza. *Patience* tells the story of Jonah and the whale, moralized as a lesson in submission to God's will; *Purity* is a loosely organized series of stories from the Bible and reflections on the virtue ("cleanness" in the Middle English) which its title denotes. *Pearl* is a dream-vision in which the narrator, stricken by the loss of the daughter that had been his pearl of great price and willfully rebellious against the faith he intellectually accepts, is led by the Pearl-maiden to a state of comparative reconciliation.

Sir Gawain and the Green Knight is an Arthurian romance; the plot of the poem, with its elements of the supernatural and of amorous intrigue, reflects both in its main outlines and in the handling of its descriptive details the treatment that the originally Celtic Arthurian legends had received at the hands of such medieval French poets as Chrétien de Troyes. As a late fourteenth-century poem, *Gawain* is a product of the end of the Middle Ages. The ideal of knightly conduct—of courage, loyalty, and courtesy—against which the poem's action is to be viewed was a long-established, though still viable, ideal, which had become subject to superficial acceptance and even satirical treatment. It may legitimately be compared to the Boy Scout ideal of conduct, similarly viable and similarly subject to ridicule, in our century.

The main story elements of which the plot of *Gawain* is composed derive ultimately from folklore, but the poet himself probably encountered them in French or Latin literary versions, and he was surely the first to combine them. The opening action of the poem retells the story of the "Beheading Game" (traditionally so called), in which an unknown challenger proposes that one of a group of warriors volunteer to cut off his head, the stroke to be repaid in kind at some future date; the hero accepts this challenge, and at the crucial moment of reprisal is spared and praised for his courage. Later action incorporates the "Temptation Story," in which an attractive woman attempts to seduce a man under circumstances in which he is bound to resist her, and the "Exchange of Winnings," in which two men agree to exchange what each has acquired during a set period of time. In the plot of *Gawain* these three stories are intricately linked: the hero, having contracted to accept a presumably mortal return stroke from the Green Knight's ax, sets out to meet him, as instructed, at the Green Chapel on New Year's Day. He is unable to find out where the Green Chapel is; instead, he comes upon a magnificent castle where he is sumptuously entertained, and later induced by his host to enter on an agreement to exchange winnings at the end of each of three successive days. The host's beautiful wife visits his bedchamber on each of the three mornings and makes amorous overtures toward him; he finally accepts from her, and conceals, a green girdle said to have the power of making its wearer invulnerable. All these plots are resolved at once in the last part of the poem as Sir Gawain and the Green Knight meet once more. When the poem ends, the most honored knight in the world, famed alike as a courageous warrior and a courteous lover, is proved fallible. His faulty act includes cowardice, since it was brought about by fear of death; covetousness, since it involved the desire to possess a valuable object; and treachery, since it resulted in a breach of faith with the host whose liegeman Gawain had sworn himself to be. To these shortcomings the poet amusingly adds a breach of courtesy as he makes this world-famed lover of women lapse momentarily into the sort of antifeminist tirade that was familiar to the medieval audience.

The *Gawain* poet, a master of juxtapositions, has constructed from these separable story elements a whole far greater than the sum of its parts. The castle in which Sir Gawain is entertained is vividly real; its architecture is in the latest continental style, its court is elegant and gay; its comfortable accommodations and sumptuous fare are as welcome as those of a modern luxury hotel. Yet it is also the mysterious castle that has appeared out of nowhere, shining and shimmering like a mirage, in direct response to Gawain's prayer to the Virgin on Christmas Eve, and it is a way-station on the road to certain death. This shadow hangs over the Christmas festivities, into whose blithe spirit the knight enters as fully as courtesy obliges him to do, and over the high comedy of the bedchamber scenes, in which he must not only refuse the lady's advances, but must manage to do so without insulting her. There is a profound psychological truth in the fact that he passes all these tests successfully and at the same time fails the most important one of all: the most dangerous temptation is that which presents itself unexpectedly, as a side issue, while we are busy resisting another. Gawain accepts the belt because he recognizes in it a marvelously appropriate device for evading imminent danger, "a jewel for his jeopardy." At the same time, his act may well seem a way of granting the importunate lady a final favor while evading her amorous invitation. Its full meaning as a cowardly, and hence covetous, grasping at life is revealed to him only later, and with stunning force.

To all this the poet has added three magnificently depicted hunting scenes in which the host, on the three successive days of Gawain's temptation, pursues the deer, the boar, and the fox. It is obvious that these episodes are thematic parallels with the bedchamber scenes, where Gawain is on the defensive and the lady figures as an entrapping huntress, and the relation between the final hunt of the fox and Gawain's ill-fated ruse in concealing the belt is equally apparent. These values are, as it were, inherent in the very presence of the three hunts in the poem, but the poet has also, by his handling of them, added to the dramatic effect of the successive episodes of the narrative. Each hunt is divided in two, enclosing the bedchamber scene of that day like the two halves of a pod. As each one opens, it presents a picture of vigorous, unhampered, and joyous activity, with the host as the central figure dominating the action. From each of these openings we move suddenly to the bed surrounded by curtains, where noise is hushed and space is confined. Nothing could more enhance our sympathetic identification with the hero, whose scope of action is as hedged about morally and socially as it is physically. Each encounter between knight and lady is followed by the conclusion of the corresponding hunt, scenes of carnage and ceremonial butchery which come with all the logic of a violent dream after dutiful constraints.

The "meaning" of the hunting scenes, finally, must be judged in terms of our experience of them, an experience in which perhaps the most salient quality is that of sheer delight: the joy inherent in physical sport at its best, when a demanding physical activity is carried on with skill, in fine weather, among loyal companions. This joy, though innocent, is of the body, bringing into play that aspect of man in which he is one with all animals. The narrator's keen sense of this joy is a part of his love of the physical world, a love manifest also in his knowledge of and delight in "all trades, their gear and tackle and trim," and in that sympathy with animals which leads him to adopt sympathetically the point of view of the hunted creatures and to imagine the suffering inflicted by wind and sleet upon the wild things of the forest. Insofar as we are made to share this attitude we are placed on the side of mortality itself, and can thus, with the Green Knight, forgive Gawain for his single act of cowardice: what he did was done not out of sensual lust but for love of life—"the less, then, to blame." In the context of this affectionate sympathy, Gawain's own violent anger at the revelation of his fault must itself be viewed with amusement, as part of his human fallibility. Yet the underlying moral is serious; the pride implicit in accepting one's own reputation has been humbled; the lesson Gawain has been taught applies *a fortiori* to the court of which he is the most honored representative and, by further extension, to all men.

The style of the poem is as traditional as the story elements making up its plot, to a degree that creates disconcerting problems for the translator. Whereas the contemporary reader looks to the contemporary poet for verbal originality and innovation, the medieval audience was accustomed to a poetry made up of traditional formulas, a diction and phraseology whose effectiveness resided in time-honored familiarity rather than the capacity to startle. And whereas the contemporary poet tends to avoid the overt expression of emotions and moral judgments, the stylistic tradition represented by *Sir Gawain and the Green Knight* calls for the frequent use of such explicitly qualitative adjectives as *noble, worthy, lovely, courteous,* and—perhaps most frequent of all—*good.* These adjectives may be used frequently and freely because, within the traditional world portrayed in this poetic style, knights are inevitably noble and worthy, ladies lovely, servants courteous, and indeed everything, aside from monsters and villainous churls, ideally good.

The formulaic style of *Gawain* cannot be discussed apart from the alliterative verse-form in which it is composed, a form which has fallen into disuse since the fourteenth and fifteenth centuries, although the language today lends itself equally well to its requirements. The alliterative tradition in Middle English is descended, with gradual modification reflecting changes in the language itself, from the alliterative tradition in Old English poetry, and this in turn is a Germanic heritage, going back to a very early body of heroic legends recited in verse while the people of the Germanic nation was still a single cultural entity in northwest Europe. The presence of a large stock of alliterating formulas in modern English, expressions like "good as gold," "the lay of the land," "the worse for wear," "to look to one's laurels," is surely connected in some way with this lost poetic inheritance.

As its name implies, the alliterating line is based on combinations of words (basically three in each line, but see the Appendix, pp. 55 ff.) beginning with the same letter. Since the traditional style in which alliterative poetry was composed was originally developed for the recounting of heroic legends, its word-stock includes numerous synonyms expressing such meanings, important for this subject matter, as "hero," "steed," "sword," "chieftain," and "battle," as well as qualitative adjectives having such meanings as "bold," "strong," and "resolute." As the alliterative style came to be used to treat the subject matter of the Romances, new groups of words were added, nouns for reference to ladies and adjectives meaning "beautiful," "gracious," "courteous," "gay." There were also numerous verbs to denote such important actions as riding, looking, and speaking. Since each word in a given group began with a different letter, the stock vocabulary, as well as the traditional phrases, constituted an important technical resource in the hands of the accomplished poet. We can view the *Gawain* poet, for example, as solving the problem of combining two nonalliterating nouns by using an alliterating adjective, as when he speaks of "a shield and a *sharp* spear" (269), or "the girdle of *green* silk" (2035).

The style of alliterative poetry is in its origins a style in which the narrator, as he tells a known story, distributes praise and blame to their appropriate recipients. In the oldest heroic poetry, the functions of narrator and historian are combined, and both narrator and historian confirm the virtues and preserve in the memory of the people the valorous feats of "our own." Ethical values are unquestioned and the tone is solemn. But *Gawain* is a poem composed late in the tradition of the chivalric romance, and it is a poem of the highest moral, as well as social, sophistication, in which both courage and courtesy are subject to test. The narrator's traditional role has not altered outwardly; he applies in the time-honored way the time-honored words of praise. He is thus literally the spokesman for the reputation of the knights of King Arthur's court, the reputation which has drawn the Green Knight to Camelot. But are their virtues literary or real? Though the narrator's manner is dignified and reassuring, the story he has to tell is not, and behind his unfailing politeness we feel that he is richly conscious of the degree of humiliation inflicted upon the assembled court by its obstreperous visitor, of Gawain's exquisite physical and social unease as he chats with the lovely lady sitting on the side of his bed. Again, is Gawain a storybook lover or is he capable of dealing adequately with the real thing? The lady continually and disconcertingly suggests that he is the former. In the mouth of the narrator of *Sir Gawain and the Green Knight*, the stock words and phrases become implements in the production of an effect that is difficult to describe, though easy to feel; they may take on a hollow sound or attract insidiously inappropriate meanings, as when the adjective *stiff*, which had in Middle English the poetic meaning "resolute" as well as its most usual modern meaning, is applied to the young King Arthur as he boyishly insists on waiting until he has seen a marvel before he joins the feast. (I have tried to produce something of the same effect by using the equally ambiguous word *stout*.)

It has seemed to me that a modern verse-translation of *Sir Gawain and the Green Knight* must fulfill certain requirements deriving from the nature of the original style. First, it must so far as possible preserve the formulaic character of the language. This not infrequently involves repetition of wording within the poem itself; for example, the poet uses the same phrase in describing the original entrance and exit of the Green Knight, and the translator ought to do the same; the poem opens and closes with much the same wording; there are verbal reminiscences of the original beheading scene in the episode at the Green Chapel, and so on. But beyond this, the style of the translation must, if possible, have something of the expectedness of the language of the fairy tale, with its "handsome princes" and "beautiful princesses," its opening "once upon a time" and its closing "they lived happily ever after"—though any suggestion of whimsy or quaintness in so adult and sophisticated a literary work would be, to say the least, out of place. In trying to meet this condition I have incorporated into the translation as many as possible of the formulas still current in the language. The reader will recognize such phrases as "tried and true," "winsome ways," "hot on his heels," and others; these have, I think, served my turn well, though many such phrases were too restricted in use to the realm of colloquial speech to be suitable in tone.

Second, the diction of the translation must, so far as possible, reflect that of the original poem. The traditional style as it appears in late Middle English embraces a wide range of kinds of words, from strictly poetic terms comparable in status to *wherefore* or *in sooth* today to words used primarily in the ordinary speech of the time, many of which have not descended into the modern language. But the style does not juxtapose discordant elements of diction for humorous effect, as the poetry of Ogden Nash, for example, does today. The level varies, but with subtle shifts of tone from solemnity to realistic vigor. I began the translation with the general notion that since the poet used words which were poetic in his time I could do the same, but I realized after a time that I was using such words where the original was colloquial, and that in any case the connotations of poetic diction for us have crucially altered. I finally used literary words only where it seemed to me that their effect was unobtrusive, and I similarly made use of distinctively colloquial words where I felt that the resultant effect was similar to that of the original. My translation thus includes both the archaic *lo!* and the colloquial *swap* (which is in the original), and I have tried to imitate the poet in modulating from one level to the other, avoiding, at one extreme, a pseudo-medieval quaintness, and, at the other, an all too homely familiarity.

Finally, a modern translation of *Sir Gawain* must, so far as possible, reproduce both the metrical variety of the original and its cumulative momentum or "swing." This aspect of the poem is discussed in some detail in the Appendix on meter, pp. 55 ff.

Like all translators of poetry, I have been faced with the basic difficulty of reproducing the sense of the poem in lines which satisfy the requirements of metrical form and, beyond this, are effective as rhythmic combinations of words. Like all translators of poetry, I have constantly had to compromise, sometimes forced away from literal rendition by the exigencies of the meter, sometimes foregoing an attractive phrase or cadence for the sake of a more faithful rendition, sometimes, I hope, finding myself able to have it both ways. I have tried to follow the poet as much in what he does not say as in what he does say, refraining from explicitness where he leads the reader, tantalizingly, to surmise. And I have done my best during the entire process of translation to attend carefully and respectfully to the exact sense of the poem at every turn, though I have inevitably had at times to decide what was essential in a given line—what must be literally reproduced at all costs—and to content myself with substitutes, hopefully of equivalent value, for the rest. Where I have been forced to deviate from the original, I have sometimes made the pleasurable discovery that in changing one line I have echoed another elsewhere in the poem.

I believe that I have in the end produced a translation more *like* the original than the others I have seen, though the success of the translation as a modern poem is for its readers to judge. It must inevitably fall short of the great achievement of the *Gawain* poet, but, like the page in the Christmas carol, I have continually found warmth and strength in treading in his footsteps.

New Haven, Connecticut   MARIE BORROFF
December, 1966

Acknowledgments

※ ≪

My first and abiding debt is to the late Professor Helge Kökeritz, and to Professors John C. Pope and E. Talbot Donaldson, who taught me Old and Middle English and the history of the English language and thus made this undertaking possible. That all three were teaching in the Graduate School of Yale University when I studied there was my great good fortune.

Professors Pope and Donaldson have made valuable criticisms, suggestions, and corrections and have given me even more valuable moral support. I am indebted to Mrs. Susan S. Addiss for her expert typing of the manuscript, and to Mrs. Addiss and Miss Anne M. Case for help with proofreading.

M. B.

SIR GAWAIN
AND THE GREEN KNIGHT

A NEW VERSE TRANSLATION

Part I

Since the siege and the assault was ceased at Troy,[1]
The walls breached and burnt down to brands and ashes,
The knight that had knotted the nets of deceit
Was impeached for his perfidy, proven most true,
It was high-born Aeneas and his haughty race   5
That since prevailed over provinces, and proudly reigned
Over well-nigh all the wealth of the West Isles.
Great Romulus to Rome repairs in haste;
With boast and with bravery builds he that city
And names it with his own name, that it now bears.   10
Ticius to Tuscany, and towers raises,
Langobard in Lombardy lays out homes,
And far over the French Sea, Felix Brutus
On many broad hills and high Britain he sets,
                              most fair.   15
            Where war and wrack and wonder
            By shifts have sojourned there,
            And bliss by turns with blunder
            In that land's lot had share.

And since this Britain was built by this baron great,   20
Bold boys bred there, in broils delighting,
That did in their day many a deed most dire.
More marvels have happened in this merry land
Than in any other I know, since that olden time,
But of those that here built, of British kings,   25
King Arthur was counted most courteous of all,
Wherefore an adventure I aim to unfold,
That a marvel of might some men think it,
And one unmatched among Arthur's wonders.
If you will listen to my lay but a little while,   30
As I heard it in hall, I shall hasten to tell
                              anew.
            As it was fashioned featly
            In tale of derring-do,
            And linked in measures meetly   35
            By letters tried and true.

1. The poet begins his story, as he later ends it, by placing the reign of King Arthur in a broad historical perspective which includes the fall of Troy. In accordance with medieval notions of history (though not all of his details can be found in the early chronicles), he visualizes Aeneas, son of the king of Troy, and his descendants, as founding a series of western kingdoms to which each gives his name. This westward movement ends with the crossing of the "French Sea" or British Channel, by Brutus, great-grandson of Aeneas, legendary founder of the kingdom of Britain. This Brutus, whom the poet calls *felix* or fortunate, is not to be confused with the Marcus Brutus of Roman history. The deceitful knight of lines 3-4 is evidently Antenor, who in Virgil's *Aeneid* is a trusted counselor, but who appears as a traitor in later versions of the Troy story.

This king lay at Camelot at Christmastide;
Many good knights and gay his guests were there,
Arrayed of the Round Table rightful brothers,
With feasting and fellowship and carefree mirth.   40
There true men contended in tournaments many,
Joined there in jousting these gentle knights,
Then came to the court for carol-dancing,
For the feast was in force full fifteen days,
With all the meat and the mirth that men could devise,   45
Such gaiety and glee, glorious to hear,
Brave din by day, dancing by night.
High were their hearts in halls and chambers,
These lords and these ladies, for life was sweet.
In peerless pleasures passed they their days,   50
The most noble knights known under Christ,
And the loveliest ladies that lived on earth ever,
And he the comeliest king, that that court holds,
For all this fair folk in their first age
                       were still.   55
          Happiest of mortal kind,
          King noblest famed of will;
          You would now go far to find
          So hardy a host on hill.

While the New Year was new, but yesternight come,   60
This fair folk at feast two-fold was served,
When the king and his company were come in together,
The chanting in chapel achieved and ended.
Clerics and all the court acclaimed the glad season,
Cried Noel anew, good news to men;   65
Then gallants gather gaily, hand-gifts to make,
Called them out clearly, claimed them by hand,
Bickered long and busily about those gifts.
Ladies laughed aloud, though losers they were,
And he that won was not angered, as well you will know.   70
All this mirth they made until meat was served;
When they had washed them worthily, they went to their seats,
The best seated above, as best it beseemed,
Guenevere the goodly queen gay in the midst
On a dais well-decked and duly arrayed   75
With costly silk curtains, a canopy over,
Of Toulouse and Turkestan tapestries rich,
All broidered and bordered with the best gems
Ever brought into Britain, with bright pennies
                       to pay.   80
          Fair queen, without a flaw,
          She glanced with eyes of grey.
          A seemlier that once he saw,
          In truth, no man could say.

But Arthur would not eat till all were served;   85

So light was his lordly heart, and a little boyish;
His life he liked lively—the less he cared
To be lying for long, or long to sit,
So busy his young blood, his brain so wild.
And also a point of pride pricked him in heart,   90
For he nobly had willed, he would never eat
On so high a holiday, till he had heard first
Of some fair feat or fray some far-borne tale,
Of some marvel of might, that he might trust,
By champions of chivalry achieved in arms,   95
Or some suppliant came seeking some single knight
To join with him in jousting, in jeopardy each
To lay life for life, and leave it to fortune
To afford him on field fair hap or other.
Such is the king's custom, when his court he holds   100
At each far-famed feast amid his fair host
                    so dear.
            The stout king stands in state
            Till a wonder shall appear;
            He leads, with heart elate,   105
            High mirth in the New Year.

So he stands there in state, the stout young king,
Talking before the high table of trifles fair.
There Gawain the good knight by Guenevere sits,
With Agravain à la dure main on her other side,   110
Both knights of renown, and nephews of the king.
Bishop Baldwin above begins the table,
And Yvain, son of Urien, ate with him there.
These few with the fair queen were fittingly served;
At the side-tables sat many stalwart knights.   115
Then the first course comes, with clamor of trumpets
That were bravely bedecked with bannerets bright,
With noise of new drums and the noble pipes.
Wild were the warbles that wakened that day
In strains that stirred many strong men's hearts.   120
There dainties were dealt out, dishes rare,
Choice fare to choose, on chargers so many
That scarce was there space to set before the people
The service of silver, with sundry meats,
                    on cloth.   125
            Each fair guest freely there
            Partakes, and nothing loth;
            Twelve dishes before each pair;
            Good beer and bright wine both.

Of the service itself I need say no more,   130
For well you will know no tittle was wanting.
Another noise and a new was well-nigh at hand,
That the lord might have leave his life to nourish;
For scarce were the sweet strains still in the hall,

And the first course come to that company fair,   135
There hurtles in at the hall-door an unknown rider,
One the greatest on ground in growth of his frame:
From broad neck to buttocks so bulky and thick,
And his loins and his legs so long and so great,
Half a giant on earth I hold him to be,   140
But believe him no less than the largest of men,
And that the seemliest in his stature to see, as he rides,
For in back and in breast though his body was grim,
His waist in its width was worthily small,
And formed with every feature in fair accord   145
                              was he.
                    Great wonder grew in hall
                    At his hue most strange to see,
                    For man and gear and all
                    Were green as green could be.   150

And in guise all of green, the gear and the man:
A coat cut close, that clung to his sides,
And a mantle to match, made with a lining
Of furs cut and fitted—the fabric was noble,
Embellished all with ermine, and his hood beside,   155
That was loosed from his locks, and laid on his shoulders.
With trim hose and tight, the same tint of green,
His great calves were girt, and gold spurs under
He bore on silk bands that embellished his heels,
And footgear well-fashioned, for riding most fit.   160
And all his vesture verily was verdant green;
Both the bosses on his belt and other bright gems
That were richly ranged on his raiment noble
About himself and his saddle, set upon silk,
That to tell half the trifles would tax my wits,   165
The butterflies and birds embroidered thereon
In green of the gayest, with many a gold thread.
The pendants of the breast-band, the princely crupper,
And the bars of the bit were brightly enameled;
The stout stirrups were green, that steadied his feet,   170
And the bows of the saddle and the side-panels both,
That gleamed all and glinted with green gems about.
The steed he bestrides of that same green
                              so bright.
                    A green horse great and thick;   175
                    A headstrong steed of might;
                    In broidered bridle quick,
                    Mount matched man aright.

Gay was this goodly man in guise all of green,
And the hair of his head to his horse suited;   180
Fair flowing tresses enfold his shoulders;
A beard big as a bush on his breast hangs,
That with his heavy hair, that from his head falls,

Was evened all about above both his elbows,
That half his arms thereunder were hid in the fashion   185
Of a king's cap-à-dos,[2] that covers his throat.
The mane of that mighty horse much to it like,
Well curled and becombed, and cunningly knotted
With filaments of fine gold amid the fair green,
Here a strand of the hair, here one of gold;   190
His tail and his foretop twin in their hue,
And bound both with a band of a bright green
That was decked adown the dock with dazzling stones
And tied tight at the top with a triple knot
Where many bells well burnished rang bright and clear.   195
Such a mount in his might, nor man on him riding,
None had seen, I dare swear, with sight in that hall
           so grand.
       As lightning quick and light
       He looked to all at hand;   200
       It seemed that no man might
       His deadly dints withstand.

Yet had he no helm, nor hauberk neither,
Nor plate, nor appurtenance appending to arms,
Nor shaft pointed sharp, nor shield for defense,   205
But in his one hand he had a holly bob
That is goodliest in green when groves are bare,
And an ax in his other, a huge and immense,
A wicked piece of work in words to expound:
The head on its haft was an ell long;   210
The spike of green steel, resplendent with gold;
The blade burnished bright, with a broad edge,
As well shaped to shear as a sharp razor;
Stout was the stave in the strong man's gripe,
That was wound all with iron to the weapon's end,   215
With engravings in green of goodliest work.
A lace lightly about, that led to a knot,
Was looped in by lengths along the fair haft,
And tassels thereto attached in a row,
With buttons of bright green, brave to behold.   220
This horseman hurtles in, and the hall enters;
Riding to the high dais, recked he no danger;
Not a greeting he gave as the guests he o'erlooked,
Nor wasted his words, but "Where is," he said,
"The captain of this crowd? Keenly I wish   225
To see that sire with sight, and to himself say
           my say."
       He swaggered all about
       To scan the host so gay;

2. The word *capados* occurs in this form in Middle English only in *Gawain*, here and in line 572. I have interpreted it, as the poet apparently did also, as *cap-à-dos*—i.e., a garment covering its wearer 'from head to back,' on the model of *cap-à-pie*, 'from head to foot,' referring to armor.

He halted, as if in doubt   230
Who in that hall held sway.

There were stares on all sides as the stranger spoke,
For much did they marvel what it might mean
That a horseman and a horse should have such a hue,
Grow green as the grass, and greener, it seemed,   235
Than green fused on gold more glorious by far.
All the onlookers eyed him, and edged nearer,
And awaited in wonder what he would do,
For many sights had they seen, but such a one never,
So that phantom and faerie the folk there deemed it,   240
Therefore chary of answer was many a champion bold,
And stunned at his strong words stone-still they sat
In a swooning silence in the stately hall.
As all were slipped into sleep, so slackened their speech
apace.   245
Not all, I think, for dread,
But some of courteous grace
Let him who was their head
Be spokesman in that place.

Then Arthur before the high dais that entrance beholds,   250
And hailed him, as behooved, for he had no fear,
And said "Fellow, in faith you have found fair welcome;
The head of this hostelry Arthur am I;
Leap lightly down, and linger, I pray,
And the tale of your intent you shall tell us after."   255
"Nay, so help me," said the other, "He that on high sits,
To tarry here any time, 'twas not mine errand;
But as the praise of you, prince, is puffed up so high,
And your court and your company are counted the best,
Stoutest under steel-gear on steeds to ride,   260
Worthiest of their works the wide world over,
And peerless to prove in passages of arms,
And courtesy here is carried to its height,
And so at this season I have sought you out.
You may be certain by the branch that I bear in hand   265
That I pass here in peace, and would part friends,
For had I come to this court on combat bent,
I have a hauberk at home, and a helm beside,
A shield and a sharp spear, shining bright,
And other weapons to wield, I ween well, to boot,   270
But as I willed no war, I wore no metal.
But if you be so bold as all men believe,
You will graciously grant the game that I ask
by right."
Arthur answer gave   275
And said, "Sir courteous knight,
If contest here you crave,
You shall not fail to fight."

"Nay, to fight, in good faith, is far from my thought;
There are about on these benches but beardless children,   280
Were I here in full arms on a haughty steed,
For measured against mine, their might is puny.
And so I call in this court for a Christmas game,
For 'tis Yule and New Year, and many young bloods about;
If any in this house such hardihood claims,   285
Be so bold in his blood, his brain so wild,
As stoutly to strike one stroke for another,
I shall give him as my gift this gisarme noble,
This ax, that is heavy enough, to handle as he likes,
And I shall bide the first blow, as bare as I sit.   290
If there be one so wilful my words to assay,
Let him leap hither lightly, lay hold of this weapon;
I quitclaim it forever, keep it as his own,
And I shall stand him a stroke, steady on this floor,
So you grant me the guerdon to give him another,   295
                sans blame.
          In a twelvemonth and a day
          He shall have of me the same;
          Now be it seen straightway
          Who dares take up the game."   300

If he astonished them at first, stiller were then
All that household in hall, the high and the low;
The stranger on his green steed stirred in the saddle,
And roisterously his red eyes he rolled all about,
Bent his bristling brows, that were bright green,   305
Wagged his beard as he watched who would arise.
When the court kept its counsel he coughed aloud,
And cleared his throat coolly, the clearer to speak:
"What, is this Arthur's house," said that horseman then,
"Whose fame is so fair in far realms and wide?   310
Where is now your arrogance and your awesome deeds,
Your valor and your victories and your vaunting words?
Now are the revel and renown of the Round Table
Overwhelmed with a word of one man's speech,
For all cower and quake, and no cut felt!"   315
With this he laughs so loud that the lord grieved;
The blood for sheer shame shot to his face,
                and pride.
          With rage his face flushed red,
          And so did all beside.   320
          Then the king as bold man bred
          Toward the stranger took a stride.

And said "Sir, now we see you will say but folly,
Which whoso has sought, it suits that he find.
No guest here is aghast of your great words.   325
Give to me your gisarme, in God's own name,
And the boon you have begged shall straight be granted."

He leaps to him lightly, lays hold of his weapon;
The green fellow on foot fiercely alights.
Now has Arthur his ax, and the haft grips,   330
And sternly stirs it about, on striking bent.
The stranger before him stood there erect,
Higher than any in the house by a head and more;
With stern look as he stood, he stroked his beard,
And with undaunted countenance drew down his coat,   335
No more moved nor dismayed for his mighty dints
Than any bold man on bench had brought him a drink
                            of wine.
                Gawain by Guenevere
                Toward the king doth now incline: 340
                "I beseech, before all here,
                That this melee may be mine."

"Would you grant me the grace," said Gawain to the king,
"To be gone from this bench and stand by you there,
If I without discourtesy might quit this board,   345
And if my liege lady misliked it not,
I would come to your counsel before your court noble.
For I find it not fit, as in faith it is known,
When such a boon is begged before all these knights,
Though you be tempted thereto, to take it on yourself   350
While so bold men about upon benches sit,
That no host under heaven is hardier of will,
Nor better brothers-in-arms where battle is joined;
I am the weakest, well I know, and of wit feeblest;
And the loss of my life would be least of any;   355
That I have you for uncle is my only praise;
My body, but for your blood, is barren of worth;
And for that this folly befits not a king,
And 'tis I that have asked it, it ought to be mine,
And if my claim be not comely let all this court judge,   360
                            in sight."
                The court assays the claim,
                And in counsel all unite
                To give Gawain the game
                And release the king outright.   365

Then the king called the knight to come to his side,
And he rose up readily, and reached him with speed,
Bows low to his lord, lays hold of the weapon,
And he releases it lightly, and lifts up his hand,
And gives him God's blessing, and graciously prays   370
That his heart and his hand may be hardy both.
"Keep, cousin," said the king, "what you cut with this day,
And if you rule it aright, then readily, I know,
You shall stand the stroke it will strike after."
Gawain goes to the guest with gisarme in hand,   375
And boldly he bides there, abashed not a whit.

Then hails he Sir Gawain, the horseman in green:
"Recount we our contract, ere you come further.
First I ask and adjure you, how you are called
That you tell me true, so that trust it I may."   380
"In good faith," said the good knight, "Gawain am I
Whose buffet befalls you, whate'er betide after,
And at this time twelvemonth take from you another
With what weapon you will, and with no man else
      alive."   385
    The other nods assent:
    "Sir Gawain, as I may thrive,
    I am wondrous well content
    That you this dint shall drive."

"Sir Gawain," said the Green Knight, "By Gog, I rejoice   390
That your fist shall fetch this favor I seek,
And you have readily rehearsed, and in right terms,
Each clause of my covenant with the king your lord,
Save that you shall assure me, sir, upon oath,
That you shall seek me yourself, wheresoever you deem   395
My lodgings may lie, and look for such wages
As you have offered me here before all this host."
"What is the way there?" said Gawain, "Where do you dwell?
I heard never of your house, by Him that made me,
Nor I know you not, knight, your name nor your court.   400
But tell me truly thereof, and teach me your name,
And I shall fare forth to find you, so far as I may,
And this I say in good certain, and swear upon oath."
"That is enough in New Year, you need say no more,"
Said the knight in the green to Gawain the noble,   405
"If I tell you true, when I have taken your knock,
And if you handily have hit, you shall hear straightway
Of my house and my home and my own name;
Then follow in my footsteps by faithful accord.
And if I spend no speech, you shall speed the better: 410
You can feast with your friends, nor further trace
      my tracks.
    Now hold your grim tool steady
    And show us how it hacks."
    "Gladly, sir; all ready,"   415
    Says Gawain; he strokes the ax.

The Green Knight upon ground girds him with care:
Bows a bit with his head, and bares his flesh:
His long lovely locks he laid over his crown,
Let the naked nape for the need be shown.   420
Gawain grips to his ax and gathers it aloft—
The left foot on the floor before him he set—
Brought it down deftly upon the bare neck,
That the shock of the sharp blow shivered the bones
And cut the flesh cleanly and clove it in twain,   425

That the blade of bright steel bit into the ground.
The head was hewn off and fell to the floor;
Many found it at their feet, as forth it rolled;
The blood gushed from the body, bright on the green,
Yet fell not the fellow, nor faltered a whit,   430
But stoutly he starts forth upon stiff shanks,
And as all stood staring he stretched forth his hand,
Laid hold of his head and heaved it aloft,
Then goes to the green steed, grasps the bridle,
Steps into the stirrup, bestrides his mount,   435
And his head by the hair in his hand holds,
And as steady he sits in the stately saddle
As he had met with no mishap, nor missing were
                          his head.
          His bulk about he haled,   440
          That fearsome body that bled;
          There were many in the court that quailed
          Before all his say was said.

For the head in his hand he holds right up;
Toward the first on the dais directs he the face,   445
And it lifted up its lids, and looked with wide eyes,
And said as much with its mouth as now you may hear:
"Sir Gawain, forget not to go as agreed,
And cease not to seek till me, sir, you find,
As you promised in the presence of these proud knights.   450
To the Green Chapel come, I charge you, to take
Such a dint as you have dealt—you have well deserved
That your neck should have a knock on New Year's morn.
The Knight of the Green Chapel I am well-known to many,
Wherefore you cannot fail to find me at last;   455
Therefore come, or be counted a recreant knight."
With a roisterous rush he flings round the reins,
Hurtles out at the hall-door, his head in his hand,
That the flint-fire flew from the flashing hooves.
Which way he went, not one of them knew   460
Nor whence he was come in the wide world
                          so fair.
          The king and Gawain gay
          Make game of the Green Knight there,
          Yet all who saw it say   465
          'Twas a wonder past compare.

Though high-born Arthur at heart had wonder,
He let no sign be seen, but said aloud
To the comely queen, with courteous speech,
"Dear dame, on this day dismay you no whit;   470
Such crafts are becoming at Christmastide,
Laughing at interludes, light songs and mirth,
Amid dancing of damsels with doughty knights.
Nevertheless of my meat now let me partake,
For I have met with a marvel, I may not deny."   475

He glanced at Sir Gawain, and gaily he said,
"Now, sir, hang up your ax, that has hewn enough,"
And over the high dais it was hung on the wall
That men in amazement might on it look,
And tell in true terms the tale of the wonder.   480
Then they turned toward the table, these two together,
The good king and Gawain, and made great feast,
With all dainties double, dishes rare,
With all manner of meat and minstrelsy both,
Such happiness wholly had they that day   485
              in hold.
          Now take care, Sir Gawain,
          That your courage wax not cold
          When you must turn again
          To your enterprise foretold.   490

Part II

This adventure had Arthur of handsels first
When young was the year, for he yearned to hear tales;
Though they wanted for words when they went to sup,
Now are fierce deeds to follow, their fists stuffed full.
Gawain was glad to begin those games in hall,   495
But if the end be harsher, hold it no wonder,
For though men are merry in mind after much drink,
A year passes apace, and proves ever new:
First things and final conform but seldom.
And so this Yule to the young year yielded place,   500
And each season ensued at its set time;
After Christmas there came the cold cheer of Lent,
When with fish and plainer fare our flesh we reprove;
But then the world's weather with winter contends:
The keen cold lessens, the low clouds lift;   505
Fresh falls the rain in fostering showers
On the face of the fields; flowers appear.
The ground and the groves wear gowns of green;
Birds build their nests, and blithely sing
That solace of all sorrow with summer comes   510
              ere long.
          And blossoms day by day
          Bloom rich and rife in throng;
          Then every grove so gay
          Of the greenwood rings with song.   515

And then the season of summer with the soft winds,
When Zephyr sighs low over seeds and shoots;
Glad is the green plant growing abroad,
When the dew at dawn drops from the leaves,
To get a gracious glance from the golden sun.   520
But harvest with harsher winds follows hard after,

Warns him to ripen well ere winter comes;
Drives forth the dust in the droughty season,
From the face of the fields to fly high in air.
Wroth winds in the welkin wrestle with the sun,   525
The leaves launch from the linden and light on the ground,
And the grass turns to gray, that once grew green.
Then all ripens and rots that rose up at first,
And so the year moves on in yesterdays many,
And winter once more, by the world's law,   530
                draws nigh.
               At Michaelmas the moon
               Hangs wintry pale in sky;
               Sir Gawain girds him soon
               For travails yet to try.   535

Till All-Hallows' Day with Arthur he dwells,
And he held a high feast to honor that knight
With great revels and rich, of the Round Table.
Then ladies lovely and lords debonair
With sorrow for Sir Gawain were sore at heart;   540
Yet they covered their care with countenance glad:
Many a mournful man made mirth for his sake.
So after supper soberly he speaks to his uncle
Of the hard hour at hand, and openly says,
"Now, liege lord of my life, my leave I take;   545
The terms of this task too well you know—
To count the cost over concerns me nothing.
But I am bound forth betimes to bear a stroke
From the grim man in green, as God may direct."
Then the first and foremost came forth in throng: 550
Yvain and Eric and others of note,
Sir Dodinal le Sauvage, the Duke of Clarence,
Lionel and Lancelot and Lucan the good,
Sir Bors and Sir Bedivere, big men both,
And many manly knights more, with Mador de la Porte.   555
All this courtly company comes to the king
To counsel their comrade, with care in their hearts;
There was much secret sorrow suffered that day
That one so good as Gawain must go in such wise
To bear a bitter blow, and his bright sword   560
                lay by.
               He said, "Why should I tarry?"
               And smiled with tranquil eye;
               "In destinies sad or merry,
               True men can but try."   565

He dwelt there all that day, and dressed in the morning;
Asked early for his arms, and all were brought.
First a carpet of rare cost was cast on the floor
Where much goodly gear gleamed golden bright;
He takes his place promptly and picks up the steel,   570

Attired in a tight coat of Turkestan silk
And a kingly cap-à-dos, closed at the throat,
That was lavishly lined with a lustrous fur.
Then they set the steel shoes on his sturdy feet
And clad his calves about with comely greaves,   575
And plate well-polished protected his knees,
Affixed with fastenings of the finest gold.
Fair cuisses enclosed, that were cunningly wrought,
His thick-thewed thighs, with thongs bound fast,
And massy chain-mail of many a steel ring   580
He bore on his body, above the best cloth,
With brace burnished bright upon both his arms,
Good couters and gay, and gloves of plate,
And all the goodly gear to grace him well
                              that tide.   585
                    His surcoat blazoned bold;
                    Sharp spurs to prick with pride;
                    And a brave silk band to hold
                    The broadsword at his side.

When he had on his arms, his harness was rich,   590
The least latchet or loop laden with gold;
So armored as he was, he heard a mass,
Honored God humbly at the high altar.
Then he comes to the king and his comrades-in-arms,
Takes his leave at last of lords and ladies,   595
And they clasped and kissed him, commending him to Christ.
By then Gringolet was girt with a great saddle
That was gaily agleam with fine gilt fringe,
New-furbished for the need with nail-heads bright;
The bridle and the bars bedecked all with gold;   600
The breast-plate, the saddlebow, the side-panels both,
The caparison and the crupper accorded in hue,
And all ranged on the red the resplendent studs
That glittered and glowed like the glorious sun.
His helm now he holds up and hastily kisses,   605
Well-closed with iron clinches, and cushioned within;
It was high on his head, with a hasp behind,
And a covering of cloth to encase the visor,
All bound and embroidered with the best gems
On broad bands of silk, and bordered with birds,   610
Parrots and popinjays preening their wings,
Lovebirds and love-knots as lavishly wrought
As many women had worked seven winters thereon,
                              entire.
                    The diadem costlier yet   615
                    That crowned that comely sire,
                    With diamonds richly set,
                    That flashed as if on fire.

Then they showed forth the shield, that shone all red,
With the pentangle portrayed in purest gold.   620
About his broad neck by the baldric he casts it,
That was meet for the man, and matched him well.
And why the pentangle is proper to that peerless prince
I intend now to tell, though detain me it must.
It is a sign by Solomon sagely devised   625
To be a token of truth, by its title of old,
For it is a figure formed of five points,
And each line is linked and locked with the next
For ever and ever, and hence it is called
In all England, as I hear, the endless knot.   630
And well may he wear it on his worthy arms,
For ever faithful five-fold in five-fold fashion
Was Gawain in good works, as gold unalloyed,
Devoid of all villainy, with virtues adorned
                    in sight.   635
          On shield and coat in view
          He bore that emblem bright,
          As to his word most true
          And in speech most courteous knight.

And first, he was faultless in his five senses,   640
Nor found ever to fail in his five fingers,
And all his fealty was fixed upon the five wounds
That Christ got on the cross, as the creed tells;
And wherever this man in melee took part,
His one thought was of this, past all things else,   645
That all his force was founded on the five joys
That the high Queen of heaven had in her child.
And therefore, as I find, he fittingly had
On the inner part of his shield her image portrayed,
That when his look on it lighted, he never lost heart.   650
The fifth of the five fives followed by this knight
Were beneficence boundless and brotherly love
And pure mind and manners, that none might impeach,
And compassion most precious—these peerless five
Were forged and made fast in him, foremost of men.   655
Now all these five fives were confirmed in this knight,
And each linked in other, that end there was none,
And fixed to five points, whose force never failed,
Nor assembled all on a side, nor asunder either,
Nor anywhere at an end, but whole and entire   660
However the pattern proceeded or played out its course.
And so on his shining shield shaped was the knot
Royally in red gold against red gules,
That is the peerless pentangle, prized of old
                    in lore.   665
          Now armed is Gawain gay,
          And bears his lance before,

And soberly said good day,
He thought forevermore.

He struck his steed with the spurs and sped on his way   670
So fast that the flint-fire flashed from the stones.
When they saw him set forth they were sore aggrieved,
And all sighed softly, and said to each other,
Fearing for their fellow, "Ill fortune it is
That you, man, must be marred, that most are worthy!   675
His equal on this earth can hardly be found;
To have dealt more discreetly had done less harm,
And have dubbed him a duke, with all due honor.
A great leader of lords he was like to become,
And better so to have been than battered to bits,   680
Beheaded by an elf-man, for empty pride!
Who would credit that a king could be counseled so,
And caught in a cavil in a Christmas game?"
Many were the warm tears they wept from their eyes
When goodly Sir Gawain was gone from the court   685
                    that day.
            No longer he abode,
            But speedily went his way
            Over many a wandering road,
            As I heard my author say.   690

Now he rides in his array through the realm of Logres,
Sir Gawain, God knows, though it gave him small joy!
All alone must he lodge through many a long night
Where the food that he fancied was far from his plate;
He had no mate but his mount, over mountain and plain,   695
Nor man to say his mind to but almighty God,
Till he had wandered well-nigh into North Wales.
All the islands of Anglesey he holds on his left,
And follows, as he fares, the fords by the coast,
Comes over at Holy Head, and enters next   700
The Wilderness of Wirral—few were within
That had great good will toward God or man.
And earnestly he asked of each mortal he met
If he had ever heard aught of a knight all green,
Or of a Green Chapel, on ground thereabouts,   705
And all said the same, and solemnly swore
They saw no such knight all solely green
                    in hue.
            Over country wild and strange
            The knight sets off anew;   710
            Often his course must change
            Ere the Chapel comes in view.

Many a cliff must he climb in country wild;
Far off from all his friends, forlorn must he ride;
At each strand or stream where the stalwart passed   715

'Twere a marvel if he met not some monstrous foe,
And that so fierce and forbidding that fight he must.
So many were the wonders he wandered among
That to tell but the tenth part would tax my wits.
Now with serpents he wars, now with savage wolves,   720
Now with wild men of the woods, that watched from the rocks,
Both with bulls and with bears, and with boars besides,
And giants that came gibbering from the jagged steeps.
Had he not borne himself bravely, and been on God's side,
He had met with many mishaps and mortal harms.   725
And if the wars were unwelcome, the winter was worse,
When the cold clear rains rushed from the clouds
And froze before they could fall to the frosty earth.
Near slain by the sleet he sleeps in his irons
More nights than enough, among naked rocks,   730
Where clattering from the crest the cold stream ran
And hung in hard icicles high overhead.
Thus in peril and pain and predicaments dire
He rides across country till Christmas Eve,
> our knight.   735
>> And at that holy tide
>> He prays with all his might
>> That Mary may be his guide
>> Till a dwelling comes in sight.

By a mountain next morning he makes his way   740
Into a forest fastness, fearsome and wild;
High hills on either hand, with hoar woods below,
Oaks old and huge by the hundred together.
The hazel and the hawthorn were all intertwined
With rough raveled moss, that raggedly hung,   745
With many birds unblithe upon bare twigs
That peeped most piteously for pain of the cold.
The good knight on Gringolet glides thereunder
Through many a marsh and mire, a man all alone;
He feared for his default, should he fail to see   750
The service of that Sire that on that same night
Was born of a bright maid, to bring us His peace.
And therefore sighing he said, "I beseech of Thee, Lord,
And Mary, thou mildest mother so dear,
Some harborage where haply I might hear mass   755
And Thy matins tomorrow—meekly I ask it,
And thereto proffer and pray my pater and ave
> and creed."
>> He said his prayer with sighs,
>> Lamenting his misdeed;   760
>> He crosses himself, and cries
>> On Christ in his great need.

No sooner had Sir Gawain signed himself thrice
Than he was ware, in the wood, of a wondrous dwelling,

Within a moat, on a mound, bright amid boughs   765
Of many a tree great of girth that grew by the water—
A castle as comely as a knight could own,
On grounds fair and green, in a goodly park
With a palisade of palings planted about
For two miles and more, round many a fair tree.   770
The stout knight stared at that stronghold great
As it shimmered and shone amid shining leaves,
Then with helmet in hand he offers his thanks
To Jesus and Saint Julian, that are gentle both,
That in courteous accord had inclined to his prayer;   775
"Now fair harbor," said he, "I humbly beseech!"
Then he pricks his proud steed with the plated spurs,
And by chance he has chosen the chief path
That brought the bold knight to the bridge's end
                            in haste.   780
              The bridge hung high in air;
              The gates were bolted fast;
              The walls well-framed to bear
              The fury of the blast.

The man on his mount remained on the bank   785
Of the deep double moat that defended the place.
The wall went in the water wondrous deep,
And a long way aloft it loomed overhead.
It was built of stone blocks to the battlements' height,
With corbels under cornices in comeliest style;   790
Watch-towers trusty protected the gate,
With many a lean loophole, to look from within:
A better-made barbican the knight beheld never.
And behind it there hoved a great hall and fair:
Turrets rising in tiers, with tines at their tops,   795
Spires set beside them, splendidly long,
With finials well-fashioned, as filigree fine.
Chalk-white chimneys over chambers high
Gleamed in gay array upon gables and roofs;
The pinnacles in panoply, pointing in air,   800
So vied there for his view that verily it seemed
A castle cut of paper for a king's feast.
The good knight on Gringolet thought it great luck
If he could but contrive to come there within
To keep the Christmas feast in that castle fair   805
                            and bright.
              There answered to his call
              A porter most polite;
              From his station on the wall
              He greets the errant knight.   810

"Good sir," said Gawain, "Wouldst go to inquire
If your lord would allow me to lodge here a space?"
"Peter!" said the porter, "For my part, I think

So noble a knight will not want for a welcome!"
Then he bustles off briskly, and comes back straight,   815
And many servants beside, to receive him the better.
They let down the drawbridge and duly went forth
And kneeled down on their knees on the naked earth
To welcome this warrior as best they were able.
They proffered him passage—the portals stood wide—   820
And he beckoned them to rise, and rode over the bridge.
Men steadied his saddle as he stepped to the ground,
And there stabled his steed many stalwart folk.
Now come the knights and the noble squires
To bring him with bliss into the bright hall.   825
When his high helm was off, there hied forth a throng
Of attendants to take it, and see to its care;
They bore away his brand and his blazoned shield;
Then graciously he greeted those gallants each one,
And many a noble drew near, to do the knight honor.   830
All in his armor into hall he was led,
Where fire on a fair hearth fiercely blazed.
And soon the lord himself descends from his chamber
To meet with good manners the man on his floor.
He said, "To this house you are heartily welcome: 835
What is here is wholly yours, to have in your power
                              and sway."
                    "Many thanks," said Sir Gawain;
                    "May Christ your pains repay!"
                    The two embrace amain   840
                    As men well met that day.

Gawain gazed on the host that greeted him there,
And a lusty fellow he looked, the lord of that place:
A man of massive mold, and of middle age;
Broad, bright was his beard, of a beaver's hue,   845
Strong, steady his stance, upon stalwart shanks,
His face fierce as fire, fair-spoken withal,
And well-suited he seemed in Sir Gawain's sight
To be a master of men in a mighty keep.
They pass into a parlor, where promptly the host   850
Has a servant assigned him to see to his needs,
And there came upon his call many courteous folk
That brought him to a bower where bedding was noble,
With heavy silk hangings hemmed all in gold,
Coverlets and counterpanes curiously wrought,   855
A canopy over the couch, clad all with fur,
Curtains running on cords, caught to gold rings,
Woven rugs on the walls of eastern work,
And the floor, under foot, well-furnished with the same.
With light talk and laughter they loosed from him then   860
His war-dress of weight and his worthy clothes.
Robes richly wrought they brought him right soon,

To change there in chamber and choose what he would.
When he had found one he fancied, and flung it about,
Well-fashioned for his frame, with flowing skirts,   865
His face fair and fresh as the flowers of spring,
All the good folk agreed, that gazed on him then,
His limbs arrayed royally in radiant hues,
That so comely a mortal never Christ made
                              as he.   870
                    Whatever his place of birth,
                    It seemed he well might be
                    Without a peer on earth
                    In martial rivalry.

A couch before the fire, where fresh coals burned,   875
They spread for Sir Gawain splendidly now
With quilts quaintly stitched, and cushions beside,
And then a costly cloak they cast on his shoulders
Of bright silk, embroidered on borders and hems,
With furs of the finest well-furnished within,   880
And bound about with ermine, both mantle and hood;
And he sat at that fireside in sumptuous estate
And warmed himself well, and soon he waxed merry.
Then attendants set a table upon trestles broad,
And lustrous white linen they laid thereupon,   885
A saltcellar of silver, spoons of the same.
He washed himself well and went to his place,
Men set his fare before him in fashion most fit.
There were soups of all sorts, seasoned with skill,
Double-sized servings, and sundry fish,   890
Some baked, some breaded, some broiled on the coals,
Some simmered, some in stews, steaming with spice,
And with sauces to sup that suited his taste.
He confesses it a feast with free words and fair;
They requite him as kindly with courteous jests,   895
                         well-sped.
                    "Tonight you fast and pray;
                    Tomorrow we'll see you fed."
                    The knight grows wondrous gay
                    As the wine goes to his head.   900

Then at times and by turns, as at table he sat,
They questioned him quietly, with queries discreet,
And he courteously confessed that he comes from the court,
And owns him of the brotherhood of high-famed Arthur,
The right royal ruler of the Round Table,   905
And the guest by their fireside is Gawain himself,
Who has happened on their house at that holy feast.
When the name of the knight was made known to the lord,
Then loudly he laughed, so elated he was,
And the men in that household made haste with joy   910
To appear in his presence promptly that day,

That of courage ever-constant, and customs pure,
Is pattern and paragon, and praised without end:
Of all knights on earth most honored is he.
Each said solemnly aside to his brother,   915
"Now displays of deportment shall dazzle our eyes
And the polished pearls of impeccable speech;
The high art of eloquence is ours to pursue
Since the father of fine manners is found in our midst.
Great is God's grace, and goodly indeed,   920
That a guest such as Gawain he guides to us here
When men sit and sing of their Savior's birth
                    in view.
            With command of manners pure
            He shall each heart imbue;   925
            Who shares his converse, sure,
            Shall learn love's language true."

When the knight had done dining and duly arose,
The dark was drawing on; the day nigh ended.
Chaplains in chapels and churches about   930
Rang the bells aright, reminding all men
Of the holy evensong of the high feast.
The lord attends alone; his fair lady sits
In a comely closet, secluded from sight.
Gawain in gay attire goes thither soon;   935
The lord catches his coat, and calls him by name,
And has him sit beside him, and says in good faith
No guest on God's earth would he gladlier greet.
For that Gawain thanked him; the two then embraced
And sat together soberly the service through.   940
Then the lady, that longed to look on the knight,
Came forth from her closet with her comely maids.
The fair hues of her flesh, her face and her hair
And her body and her bearing were beyond praise,
And excelled the queen herself, as Sir Gawain thought.   945
He goes forth to greet her with gracious intent;
Another lady led her by the left hand
That was older than she—an ancient, it seemed,
And held in high honor by all men about.
But unlike to look upon, those ladies were,   950
For if the one was fresh, the other was faded:
Bedecked in bright red was the body of one;
Flesh hung in folds on the face of the other;
On one a high headdress, hung all with pearls;
Her bright throat and bosom fair to behold,   955
Fresh as the first snow fallen upon hills;
A wimple the other one wore round her throat;
Her swart chin well swaddled, swathed all in white;
Her forehead enfolded in flounces of silk
That framed a fair fillet, of fashion ornate,   960

And nothing bare beneath save the black brows,
The two eyes and the nose, the naked lips,
And they unsightly to see, and sorrily bleared.
A beldame, by God, she may well be deemed,
of pride! 965
She was short and thick of waist,
Her buttocks round and wide;
More toothsome, to his taste,
Was the beauty by her side.

When Gawain had gazed on that gay lady, 970
With leave of her lord, he politely approached;
To the elder in homage he humbly bows;
The lovelier he salutes with a light embrace.
He claims a comely kiss, and courteously he speaks;
They welcome him warmly, and straightway he asks 975
To be received as their servant, if they so desire.
They take him between them; with talking they bring him
Beside a bright fire; bade then that spices
Be freely fetched forth, to refresh them the better,
And the good wine therewith, to warm their hearts. 980
The lord leaps about in light-hearted mood;
Contrives entertainments and timely sports;
Takes his hood from his head and hangs it on a spear,
And offers him openly the honor thereof
Who should promote the most mirth at that Christmas feast; 985
"And I shall try for it, trust me—contend with the best,
Ere I go without my headgear by grace of my friends!"
Thus with light talk and laughter the lord makes merry
To gladden the guest he had greeted in hall
that day. 990
At the last he called for light
The company to convey;
Gawain says goodnight
And retires to bed straightway.

On the morn when each man is mindful in heart 995
That God's son was sent down to suffer our death,
No household but is blithe for His blessed sake;
So was it there on that day, with many delights.
Both at larger meals and less they were lavishly served
By doughty lads on dais, with delicate fare; 1000
The old ancient lady, highest she sits;
The lord at her left hand leaned, as I hear;
Sir Gawain in the center, beside the gay lady,
Where the food was brought first to that festive board,
And thence throughout the hall, as they held most fit, 1005
To each man was offered in order of rank.
There was meat, there was mirth, there was much joy,
That to tell all the tale would tax my wits,
Though I pained me, perchance, to paint it with care;

But yet I know that our knight and the noble lady   1010
Were accorded so closely in company there,
With the seemly solace of their secret words,
With speeches well-sped, spotless and pure,
That each prince's pastime their pleasures far
                         outshone.   1015
                    Sweet pipes beguile their cares,
                    And the trumpet of martial tone;
                    Each tends his affairs
                    And those two tend their own.

That day and all the next, their disport was noble,   1020
And the third day, I think, pleased them no less;
The joys of St. John's Day were justly praised,
And were the last of their like for those lords and ladies;
Then guests were to go in the gray morning,
Wherefore they whiled the night away with wine and
     with mirth,   1025
Moved to the measures of many a blithe carol;
At last, when it was late, took leave of each other,
Each one of those worthies, to wend his way.
Gawain bids goodbye to his goodly host
Who brings him to his chamber, the chimney beside,   1030
And detains him in talk, and tenders his thanks
And holds it an honor to him and his people
That he has harbored in his house at that holy time
And embellished his abode with his inborn grace.
"As long as I may live, my luck is the better   1035
That Gawain was my guest at God's own feast!"
"Noble sir," said the knight, "I cannot but think
All the honor is your own—may heaven requite it!
And your man to command I account myself here
As I am bound and beholden, and shall be, come   1040
                         what may."
                    The lord with all his might
                    Entreats his guest to stay;
                    Brief answer makes the knight:
                    Next morning he must away.   1045

Then the lord of that land politely inquired
What dire affair had forced him, at that festive time,
So far from the king's court to fare forth alone
Ere the holidays wholly had ended in hall.
"In good faith," said Gawain, "you have guessed the truth: 1050
On a high errand and urgent I hastened away,
For I am summoned by myself to seek for a place—
I would I knew whither, or where it might be!
Far rather would I find it before the New Year
Than own the land of Logres, so help me our Lord!   1055
Wherefore, sir, in friendship this favor I ask,
That you say in sober earnest, if something you know
Of the Green Chapel, on ground far or near,

Or the lone knight that lives there, of like hue of green.
A certain day was set by assent of us both   1060
To meet at that landmark, if I might last,
And from now to the New Year is nothing too long,
And I would greet the Green Knight there, would God but allow,
More gladly, by God's Son, than gain the world's wealth!
And I must set forth to search, as soon as I may;   1065
To be about the business I have but three days
And would as soon sink down dead as desist from my errand."
Then smiling said the lord, "Your search, sir, is done,
For we shall see you to that site by the set time.
Let Gawain grieve no more over the Green Chapel;   1070
You shall be in your own bed, in blissful ease,
All the forenoon, and fare forth the first of the year,
And make the goal by midmorn, to mind your affairs,
                         no fear!
            Tarry till the fourth day   1075
            And ride on the first of the year.
            We shall set you on your way;
            It is not two miles from here."

Then Gawain was glad, and gleefully he laughed:
"Now I thank you for this, past all things else!   1080
Now my goal is here at hand! With a glad heart I shall
Both tarry, and undertake any task you devise."
Then the host seized his arm and seated him there;
Let the ladies be brought, to delight them the better,
And in fellowship fair by the fireside they sit;   1085
So gay waxed the good host, so giddy his words,
All waited in wonder what next he would say.
Then he stares on the stout knight, and sternly he speaks:
"You have bound yourself boldly my bidding to do——
Will you stand by that boast, and obey me this once?"   1090
"I shall do so indeed," said the doughty knight;
"While I lie in your lodging, your laws will I follow."
"As you have had," said the host, "many hardships abroad
And little sleep of late, you are lacking, I judge,
Both in nourishment needful and nightly rest;   1095
You shall lie abed late in your lofty chamber
Tomorrow until mass, and meet then to dine
When you will, with my wife, who will sit by your side
And talk with you at table, the better to cheer
                         our guest.   1100
            A-hunting I will go
            While you lie late and rest."
            The knight, inclining low,
            Assents to each behest.

"And Gawain," said the good host, "agree now to this: 1105
Whatever I win in the woods I will give you at eve,
And all you have earned you must offer to me;

Swear now, sweet friend, to swap as I say,
Whether hands, in the end, be empty or better."
"By God," said Sir Gawain, "I grant it forthwith!   1110
If you find the game good, I shall gladly take part."
"Let the bright wine be brought, and our bargain is done,"
Said the lord of that land—the two laughed together.
Then they drank and they dallied and doffed all constraint,
These lords and these ladies, as late as they chose,   1115
And then with gaiety and gallantries and graceful adieux
They talked in low tones, and tarried at parting.
With compliments comely they kiss at the last;
There were brisk lads about with blazing torches
To see them safe to bed, for soft repose   1120
                    long due.
              Their covenants, yet awhile,
              They repeat, and pledge anew;
              That lord could well beguile
              Men's hearts, with mirth in view.   1125

Part III

Long before daylight they left their beds;
Guests that wished to go gave word to their grooms,
And they set about briskly to bind on saddles,
Tend to their tackle, tie up trunks.
The proud lords appear, appareled to ride,   1130
Leap lightly astride, lay hold of their bridles,
Each one on his way to his worthy house.
The liege lord of the land was not the last
Arrayed there to ride, with retainers many;
He had a bite to eat when he had heard mass;   1135
With horn to the hills he hastens amain.
By the dawn of that day over the dim earth,
Master and men were mounted and ready.
Then they harnessed in couples the keen-scented hounds,
Cast wide the kennel-door and called them forth,   1140
Blew upon their bugles bold blasts three;
The dogs began to bay with a deafening din,
And they quieted them quickly and called them to heel,
A hundred brave huntsmen, as I have heard tell,
                    together.   1145
              Men at stations meet;
              From the hounds they slip the tether;
              The echoing horns repeat,
              Clear in the merry weather.

At the clamor of the quest, the quarry trembled;   1150
Deer dashed through the dale, dazed with dread;
Hastened to the high ground, only to be
Turned back by the beaters, who boldly shouted.

They harmed not the harts, with their high heads,
Let the bucks go by, with their broad antlers,   1155
For it was counted a crime, in the close season,
If a man of that demesne should molest the male deer.
The hinds were headed up, with "Hey!" and "Ware!"
The does with great din were driven to the valleys.
Then you were ware, as they went, of the whistling of arrows;   1160
At each bend under boughs the bright shafts flew
That tore the tawny hide with their tapered heads.
Ah! they bray and they bleed, on banks they die,
And ever the pack pell-mell comes panting behind;
Hunters with shrill horns hot on their heels—   1165
Like the cracking of cliffs their cries resounded.
What game got away from the gallant archers
Was promptly picked off at the posts below
When they were harried on the heights and herded to the streams:
The watchers were so wary at the waiting-stations,   1170
And the greyhounds so huge, that eagerly snatched,
And finished them off as fast as folk could see
                          with sight.
              The lord, now here, now there,
              Spurs forth in sheer delight.   1175
              And drives, with pleasures rare,
              The day to the dark night.

So the lord in the linden-wood leads the hunt
And Gawain the good knight in gay bed lies,
Lingered late alone, till daylight gleamed,   1180
Under coverlet costly, curtained about.
And as he slips into slumber, slyly there comes
A little din at his door, and the latch lifted,
And he holds up his heavy head out of the clothes;
A corner of the curtain he caught back a little   1185
And waited there warily, to see what befell.
Lo! it was the lady, loveliest to behold,
That drew the door behind her deftly and still
And was bound for his bed—abashed was the knight,
And laid his head low again in likeness of sleep;   1190
And she stepped stealthily, and stole to his bed,
Cast aside the curtain and came within,
And set herself softly on the bedside there,
And lingered at her leisure, to look on his waking.
The fair knight lay feigning for a long while,   1195
Conning in his conscience what his case might
Mean or amount to—a marvel he thought it.
But yet he said within himself, "More seemly it were
To try her intent by talking a little."
So he started and stretched, as startled from sleep,   1200
Lifts wide his lids in likeness of wonder,
And signs himself swiftly, as safer to be,
                          with art.

> Sweetly does she speak
> And kindling glances dart,   1205
> Blent white and red on cheek
> And laughing lips apart.

"Good morning, Sir Gawain," said that gay lady,
"A slack sleeper you are, to let one slip in!
Now you are taken in a trice—a truce we must make,   1210
Or I shall bind you in your bed, of that be assured."
Thus laughing lightly that lady jested.
"Good morning, good lady," said Gawain the blithe,
"Be it with me as you will; I am well content!
For I surrender myself, and sue for your grace,   1215
And that is best, I believe, and behooves me now."
Thus jested in answer that gentle knight.
"But if, lovely lady, you misliked it not,
And were pleased to permit your prisoner to rise,
I should quit this couch and accoutre me better,   1220
And be clad in more comfort for converse here."
"Nay, not so, sweet sir," said the smiling lady;
"You shall not rise from your bed; I direct you better:
I shall hem and hold you on either hand,
And keep company awhile with my captive knight.   1225
For as certain as I sit here, Sir Gawain you are,
Whom all the world worships, whereso you ride;
Your honor, your courtesy are highest acclaimed
By lords and by ladies, by all living men;
And lo! we are alone here, and left to ourselves: 1230
My lord and his liegemen are long departed,
The household asleep, my handmaids too,
The door drawn, and held by a well-driven bolt,
And since I have in this house him whom all love,
I shall while the time away with mirthful speech   1235
> at will.
> My body is here at hand,
> Your each wish to fulfill;
> Your servant to command
> I am, and shall be still."   1240

"In good faith," said Gawain, "my gain is the greater,
Though I am not he of whom you have heard;
To arrive at such reverence as you recount here
I am one all unworthy, and well do I know it.
By heaven, I would hold me the happiest of men   1245
If by word or by work I once might aspire
To the prize of your praise—'twere a pure joy!"
"In good faith, Sir Gawain," said that gay lady,
"The well-proven prowess that pleases all others,
Did I scant or scout it, 'twere scarce becoming.   1250
But there are ladies, believe me, that had liefer far
Have thee here in their hold, as I have today,

To pass an hour in pastime with pleasant words,
Assuage all their sorrows and solace their hearts,
Than much of the goodly gems and gold they possess.   1255
But laud be to the Lord of the lofty skies,
For here in my hands all hearts' desire
     doth lie."
    Great welcome got he there
    From the lady who sat him by;   1260
    With fitting speech and fair
    The good knight makes reply.

"Madame," said the merry man, "Mary reward you!
For in good faith, I find your beneficence noble.
And the fame of fair deeds runs far and wide,   1265
But the praise you report pertains not to me,
But comes of your courtesy and kindness of heart."
"By the high Queen of heaven" (said she) "I count it not so,
For were I worth all the women in this world alive,
And all wealth and all worship were in my hands,   1270
And I should hunt high and low, a husband to take,
For the nurture I have noted in thee, knight, here,
The comeliness and courtesies and courtly mirth—
And so I had ever heard, and now hold it true—
No other on this earth should have me for wife."   1275
"You are bound to a better man," the bold knight said,
"Yet I prize the praise you have proffered me here,
And soberly your servant, my sovereign I hold you,
And acknowledge me your knight, in the name of Christ."
So they talked of this and that until 'twas nigh noon,   1280
And ever the lady languishing in likeness of love.
With feat words and fair he framed his defence,
For were she never so winsome, the warrior had
The less will to woo, for the wound that his bane
     must be.   1285
    He must bear the blinding blow,
    For such is fate's decree;
    The lady asks leave to go;
    He grants it full and free.

Then she gaily said goodbye, and glanced at him, laughing,   1290
And as she stood, she astonished him with a stern speech:
"Now may the Giver of all good words these glad hours repay!
But our guest is not Gawain—forgot is that thought."
"How so?" said the other, and asks in some haste,
For he feared he had been at fault in the forms of his speech.   1295
But she held up her hand, and made answer thus:
"So good a knight as Gawain is given out to be,
And the model of fair demeanor and manners pure,
Had he lain so long at a lady's side,
Would have claimed a kiss, by his courtesy,   1300
Through some touch or trick of phrase at some tale's end."

Said Gawain, "Good lady, I grant it at once!
I shall kiss at your command, as becomes a knight,
And more, lest you mislike, so let be, I pray."
With that she turns toward him, takes him in her arms,   1305
Leans down her lovely head, and lo! he is kissed.
They commend each other to Christ with comely words,
He sees her forth safely, in silence they part,
And then he lies no later in his lofty bed,
But calls to his chamberlain, chooses his clothes,   1310
Goes in those garments gladly to mass,
Then takes his way to table, where attendants wait,
And made merry all day, till the moon rose
                    in view
            Was never knight beset   1315
            'Twixt worthier ladies two:
            The crone and the coquette;
            Fair pastimes they pursue.

And the lord of the land rides late and long,
Hunting the barren hind over the broad heath.   1320
He had slain such a sum, when the sun sank low,
Of does and other deer, as would dizzy one's wits.
Then they trooped in together in triumph at last,
And the count of the quarry quickly they take.
The lords lent a hand with their liegemen many,   1325
Picked out the plumpest and put them together
And duly dressed the deer, as the deed requires.
Some were assigned the assay of the fat:
Two fingers'-width fully they found on the leanest.
Then they slit the slot open and searched out the paunch,   1330
Trimmed it with trencher-knives and tied it up tight.
They flayed the fair hide from the legs and trunk,
Then broke open the belly and laid bare the bowels,
Deftly detaching and drawing them forth.
And next at the neck they neatly parted   1335
The weasand from the windpipe, and cast away the guts.
At the shoulders with sharp blades they showed their skill,
Boning them from beneath, lest the sides be marred;
They breached the broad breast and broke it in twain,
And again at the gullet they begin with their knives,   1340
Cleave down the carcass clear to the breach;
Two tender morsels they take from the throat,
Then round the inner ribs they rid off a layer
And carve out the kidney-fat, close to the spine,
Hewing down to the haunch, that all hung together,   1345
And held it up whole, and hacked it free,
And this they named the numbles, that knew such terms
                    of art.
            They divide the crotch in two,
            And straightway then they start   1350

> To cut the backbone through
> And cleave the trunk apart.

With hard strokes they hewed off the head and the neck,
Then swiftly from the sides they severed the chine,
And the corbie's bone they cast on a branch.   1355
Then they pierced the plump sides, impaled either one
With the hock of the hind foot, and hung it aloft,
To each person his portion most proper and fit.
On a hide of a hind the hounds they fed
With the liver and the lights, the leathery paunches,   1360
And bread soaked in blood well blended therewith.
High horns and shrill set hounds a-baying,
Then merrily with their meat they make their way home,
Blowing on their bugles many a brave blast.
Ere dark had descended, that doughty band   1365
Was come within the walls where Gawain waits
>   at leisure.
>   Bliss and hearth-fire bright
>   Await the master's pleasure;
>   When the two men met that night,   1370
>   Joy surpassed all measure.

Then the host in the hall his household assembles,
With the dames of high degree and their damsels fair.
In the presence of the people, a party he sends
To convey him his venison in view of the knight.   1375
And in high good-humor he hails him then,
Counts over the kill, the cuts on the tallies,
Holds high the hewn ribs, heavy with fat.
"What think you, sir, of this? Have I thriven well?
Have I won with my woodcraft a worthy prize?"   1380
"In good earnest," said Gawain, "this game is the finest
I have seen in seven years in the season of winter."
"And I give it to you, Gawain," said the goodly host,
"For according to our covenant, you claim it as your own."
"That is so," said Sir Gawain, "the same say I: 1385
What I worthily have won within these fair walls,
Herewith I as willingly award it to you."
He embraces his broad neck with both his arms,
And confers on him a kiss in the comeliest style.
"Have here my profit, it proved no better;   1390
Ungrudging do I grant it, were it greater far."
"Such a gift," said the good host, "I gladly accept—
Yet it might be all the better, would you but say
Where you won this same award, by your wits alone."
"That was no part of the pact; press me no further,   1395
For you have had what behooves; all other claims
>   forbear."
>   With jest and compliment
>   They conversed, and cast off care;

To the table soon they went; 1400
Fresh dainties wait them there.

And then by the chimney-side they chat at their ease;
The best wine was brought them, and bounteously served;
And after in their jesting they jointly accord
To do on the second day the deeds of the first: 1405
That the two men should trade, betide as it may,
What each had taken in, at eve when they met.
They seal the pact solemnly in sight of the court;
Their cups were filled afresh to confirm the jest;
Then at last they took their leave, for late was the hour, 1410
Each to his own bed hastening away.
Before the barnyard cock had crowed but thrice
The lord had leapt from his rest, his liegemen as well.
Both of mass and their meal they made short work:
By the dim light of dawn they were deep in the woods 1415
away.

With huntsmen and with horns
Over plains they pass that day;
They release, amid the thorns,
Swift hounds that run and bay. 1420

Soon some were on a scent by the side of a marsh;
When the hounds opened cry, the head of the hunt
Rallied them with rough words, raised a great noise.
The hounds that had heard it came hurrying straight
And followed along with their fellows, forty together. 1425
Then such a clamor and cry of coursing hounds
Arose, that the rocks resounded again.
Hunters exhorted them with horn and with voice;
Then all in a body bore off together
Between a mere in the marsh and a menacing crag, 1430
To a rise where the rock stood rugged and steep,
And boulders lay about, that blocked their approach.
Then the company in consort closed on their prey:
They surrounded the rise and the rocks both,
For well they were aware that it waited within, 1435
The beast that the bloodhounds boldly proclaimed.
Then they beat on the bushes and bade him appear,
And he made a murderous rush in the midst of them all;
The best of all boars broke from his cover,
That had ranged long unrivaled, a renegade old, 1440
For of tough-brawned boars he was biggest far,
Most grim when he grunted—then grieved were many,
For three at the first thrust he threw to the earth,
And dashed away at once without more damage.
With "Hi!" "Hi!" and "Hey!" "Hey!" the others followed, 1445
Had horns at their lips, blew high and clear.
Merry was the music of men and of hounds

That were bound after this boar, his bloodthirsty heart
to quell.
Often he stands at bay,   1450
Then scatters the pack pell-mell;
He hurts the hounds, and they
Most dolefully yowl and yell.

Men then with mighty bows moved in to shoot,
Aimed at him with their arrows and often hit,   1455
But the points had no power to pierce through his hide,
And the barbs were brushed aside by his bristly brow;
Though the shank of the shaft shivered in pieces,
The head hopped away, wheresoever it struck.
But when their stubborn strokes had stung him at last,   1460
Then, foaming in his frenzy, fiercely he charges,
Hies at them headlong that hindered his flight,
And many feared for their lives, and fell back a little.
But the lord on a lively horse leads the chase;
As a high-mettled huntsman his horn he blows;   1465
He sounds the assembly and sweeps through the brush,
Pursuing this wild swine till the sunlight slanted.
All day with this deed they drive forth the time
While our lone knight so lovesome lies in his bed,
Sir Gawain safe at home, in silken bower   1470
so gay.
The lady, with guile in heart,
Came early where he lay;
She was at him with all her art
To turn his mind her way.   1475

She comes to the curtain and coyly peeps in;
Gawain thought it good to greet her at once,
And she richly repays him with her ready words,
Settles softly at his side, and suddenly she laughs,
And with a gracious glance, she begins on him thus: 1480
"Sir, if you be Gawain, it seems a great wonder—
A man so well-meaning, and mannerly disposed,
And cannot act in company as courtesy bids,
And if one takes the trouble to teach him, 'tis all in vain.
That lesson learned lately is lightly forgot,   1485
Though I painted it as plain as my poor wit allowed."
"What lesson, dear lady?" he asked all alarmed;
"I have been much to blame, if your story be true."
"Yet my counsel was of kissing," came her answer then,
"Where favor has been found, freely to claim   1490
As accords with the conduct of courteous knights."
"My dear," said the doughty man, "dismiss that thought;
Such freedom, I fear, might offend you much;
It were rude to request if the right were denied."
"But none can deny you," said the noble dame,   1495
"You are stout enough to constrain with strength, if you choose,

Were any so ungracious as to grudge you aught."
"By heaven," said he, "you have answered well,
But threats never throve among those of my land,
Nor any gift not freely given, good though it be.   1500
I am yours to command, to kiss when you please;
You may lay on as you like, and leave off at will."
> With this,
> The lady lightly bends
> And graciously gives him a kiss;   1505
> The two converse as friends
> Of true love's trials and bliss.

"I should like, by your leave," said the lovely lady,
"If it did not annoy you, to know for what cause
So brisk and so bold a young blood as you,   1510
And acclaimed for all courtesies becoming a knight—
And name what knight you will, they are noblest esteemed
For loyal faith in love, in life as in story;
For to tell the tribulations of these true hearts,
Why, 'tis the very title and text of their deeds,   1515
How bold knights for beauty have braved many a foe,
Suffered heavy sorrows out of secret love,
And then valorously avenged them on villainous churls
And made happy ever after the hearts of their ladies.
And you are the noblest knight known in your time;   1520
No household under heaven but has heard of your fame,
And here by your side I have sat for two days
Yet never has a fair phrase fallen from your lips
Of the language of love, not one little word!
And you, that with sweet vows sway women's hearts,   1525
Should show your winsome ways, and woo a young thing,
And teach by some tokens the craft of true love.
How! are you artless, whom all men praise?
Or do you deem me so dull, or deaf to such words?
> Fie! Fie!   1530
> In hope of pastimes new
> I have come where none can spy;
> Instruct me a little, do,
> While my husband is not nearby."

"God love you, gracious lady!" said Gawain then;   1535
"It is a pleasure surpassing, and a peerless joy,
That one so worthy as you would willingly come
And take the time and trouble to talk with your knight
And content you with his company—it comforts my heart.
But to take to myself the task of telling of love,   1540
And touch upon its texts, and treat of its themes
To one that, I know well, wields more power
In that art, by a half, than a hundred such
As I am where I live, or am like to become,
It were folly, fair dame, in the first degree!   1545

In all that I am able, my aim is to please,
As in honor behooves me, and am evermore
Your servant heart and soul, so save me our Lord!"
Thus she tested his temper and tried many a time,
Whatever her true intent, to entice him to sin,   1550
But so fair was his defense that no fault appeared,
Nor evil on either hand, but only bliss
                    they knew.
            They linger and laugh awhile;
            She kisses the knight so true,   1555
            Takes leave in comeliest style
            And departs without more ado.

Then he rose from his rest and made ready for mass,
And then a meal was set and served, in sumptuous style;
He dallied at home all day with the dear ladies,   1560
But the lord lingered late at his lusty sport;
Pursued his sorry swine, that swerved as he fled,
And bit asunder the backs of the best of his hounds
When they brought him to bay, till the bowmen appeared
And soon forced him forth, though he fought for dear life,   1565
So sharp were the shafts they shot at him there.
But yet the boldest drew back from his battering head,
Till at last he was so tired he could travel no more,
But in as much haste as he might, he makes his retreat
To a rise on rocky ground, by a rushing stream.   1570
With the bank at his back he scrapes the bare earth,
The froth foams at his jaws, frightful to see.
He whets his white tusks—then weary were all
Those hunters so hardy that hoved round about
Of aiming from afar, but ever they mistrust   1575
                    his mood.
            He had hurt so many by then
            That none had hardihood
            To be torn by his tusks again,
            That was brainsick, and out for blood.   1580

Till the lord came at last on his lofty steed,
Beheld him there at bay before all his folk;
Lightly he leaps down, leaves his courser,
Bares his bright sword, and boldly advances;
Straight into the stream he strides towards his foe.   1585
The wild thing was wary of weapon and man;
His hackles rose high; so hotly he snorts
That many watched with alarm, lest the worst befall.
The boar makes for the man with a mighty bound
So that he and his hunter came headlong together   1590
Where the water ran wildest—the worse for the beast,
For the man, when they first met, marked him with care,
Sights well the slot, slips in the blade,
Shoves it home to the hilt, and the heart shattered,

And he falls in his fury and floats down the water,   1595
              ill-sped.
          Hounds hasten by the score
          To maul him, hide and head;
          Men drag him in to shore
          And dogs pronounce him dead.   1600

With many a brave blast they boast of their prize,
All hallooed in high glee, that had their wind;
The hounds bayed their best, as the bold men bade
That were charged with chief rank in that chase of renown.
Then one wise in woodcraft, and worthily skilled,   1605
Began to dress the boar in becoming style:
He severs the savage head and sets it aloft,
Then rends the body roughly right down the spine;
Takes the bowels from the belly, broils them on coals,
Blends them well with bread to bestow on the hounds.   1610
Then he breaks out the brawn in fair broad flitches,
And the innards to be eaten in order he takes.
The two sides, attached to each other all whole,
He suspended from a spar that was springy and tough;
And so with this swine they set out for home;   1615
The boar's head was borne before the same man
That had stabbed him in the stream with his strong arm,
              right through.
          He thought it long indeed
          Till he had the knight in view;   1620
          At his call, he comes with speed
          To claim his payment due.

The lord laughed aloud, with many a light word,
When he greeted Sir Gawain—with good cheer he speaks.
They fetch the fair dames and the folk of the house;   1625
He brings forth the brawn, and begins the tale
Of the great length and girth, the grim rage as well,
Of the battle of the boar they beset in the wood.
The other man meetly commended his deeds
And praised well the prize of his princely sport,   1630
For the brawn of that boar, the bold knight said,
And the sides of that swine surpassed all others.
Then they handled the huge head; he owns it a wonder,
And eyes it with abhorrence, to heighten his praise.
"Now, Gawain," said the good man, "this game becomes yours   1635
By those fair terms we fixed, as you know full well."
"That is true," returned the knight, "and trust me, fair friend,
All my gains, as agreed, I shall give you forthwith."
He clasps him and kisses him in courteous style,
Then serves him with the same fare a second time.   1640
"Now we are even," said he, "at this evening feast,
And clear is every claim incurred here to date,
              and debt."

"By Saint Giles!" the host replies,
"You're the best I ever met!   1645
If your profits are all this size,
We'll see you wealthy yet!"

Then attendants set tables on trestles about,
And laid them with linen; light shone forth,
Wakened along the walls in waxen torches.   1650
The service was set and the supper brought;
Royal were the revels that rose then in hall
At that feast by the fire, with many fair sports:
Amid the meal and after, melody sweet,
Carol-dances comely and Christmas songs,   1655
With all the mannerly mirth my tongue may describe.
And ever our gallant knight beside the gay lady;
So uncommonly kind and complaisant was she,
With sweet stolen glances, that stirred his stout heart,
That he was at his wits' end, and wondrous vexed;   1660
But he could not in conscience her courtship repay,
Yet took pains to please her, though the plan might
                      go wrong.
          When they to heart's delight
          Had reveled there in throng,   1665
          To his chamber he calls the knight,
          And thither they go along.

And there they dallied and drank, and deemed it good sport
To enact their play anew on New Year's Eve,
But Gawain asked again to go on the morrow,   1670
For the time until his tryst was not two days.
The host hindered that, and urged him to stay,
And said, "On my honor, my oath here I take
That you shall get to the Green Chapel to begin your chores
By dawn on New Year's Day, if you so desire.   1675
Wherefore lie at your leisure in your lofty bed,
And I shall hunt hereabouts, and hold to our terms,
And we shall trade winnings when once more we meet,
For I have tested you twice, and true have I found you;
Now think this tomorrow: the third pays for all;   1680
Be we merry while we may, and mindful of joy,
For heaviness of heart can be had for the asking."
This is gravely agreed on and Gawain will stay.
They drink a last draught and with torches depart
                      to rest.   1685
          To bed Sir Gawain went;
          His sleep was of the best;
          The lord, on his craft intent,
          Was early up and dressed.

After mass, with his men, a morsel he takes;   1690
Clear and crisp the morning; he calls for his mount;

The folk that were to follow him afield that day
Were high astride their horses before the hall gates.
Wondrous fair were the fields, for the frost was light;
The sun rises red amid radiant clouds,   1695
Sails into the sky, and sends forth his beams.
They let loose the hounds by a leafy wood;
The rocks all around re-echo to their horns;
Soon some have set off in pursuit of the fox,
Cast about with craft for a clearer scent;   1700
A young dog yaps, and is yelled at in turn;
His fellows fall to sniffing, and follow his lead,
Running in a rabble on the right track,
And he scampers all before; they discover him soon,
And when they see him with sight they pursue him the faster,   1705
Railing at him rudely with a wrathful din.
Often he reverses over rough terrain,
Or loops back to listen in the lee of a hedge;
At last, by a little ditch, he leaps over the brush,
Comes into a clearing at a cautious pace,   1710
Then he thought through his wiles to have thrown off the hounds
Till he was ware, as he went, of a waiting-station
Where three athwart his path threatened him at once,
        all gray.
        Quick as a flash he wheels   1715
        And darts off in dismay;
        With hard luck at his heels
        He is off to the wood away.

Then it was heaven on earth to hark to the hounds
When they had come on their quarry, coursing together!   1720
Such harsh cries and howls they hurled at his head
As all the cliffs with a crash had come down at once.
Here he was hailed, when huntsmen met him;
Yonder they yelled at him, yapping and snarling;
There they cried "Thief!" and threatened his life,   1725
And ever the harriers at his heels, that he had no rest.
Often he was menaced when he made for the open,
And often rushed in again, for Reynard was wily;
And so he leads them a merry chase, the lord and his men,
In this manner on the mountains, till midday or near,   1730
While our hero lies at home in wholesome sleep
Within the comely curtains on the cold morning.
But the lady, as love would allow her no rest,
And pursuing ever the purpose that pricked her heart,
Was awake with the dawn, and went to his chamber   1735
In a fair flowing mantle that fell to the earth,
All edged and embellished with ermines fine;
No hood on her head, but heavy with gems
Were her fillet and the fret that confined her tresses;
Her face and her fair throat freely displayed;   1740

Her bosom all but bare, and her back as well.
She comes in at the chamber-door, and closes it with care,
Throws wide a window—then waits no longer,
But hails him thus airily with her artful words,
with cheer: 1745
"Ah, man, how can you sleep?
The morning is so clear!"
Though dreams have drowned him deep,
He cannot choose but hear.

Deep in his dreams he darkly mutters 1750
As a man may that mourns, with many grim thoughts
Of that day when destiny shall deal him his doom
When he greets his grim host at the Green Chapel
And must bow to his buffet, bating all strife.
But when he sees her at his side he summons his wits, 1755
Breaks from the black dreams, and blithely answers.
That lovely lady comes laughing sweet,
Sinks down at his side, and salutes him with a kiss.
He accords her fair welcome in courtliest style;
He sees her so glorious, so gaily attired, 1760
So faultless her features, so fair and so bright,
His heart swelled swiftly with surging joys.
They melt into mirth with many a fond smile,
And there was bliss beyond telling between those two,
at height. 1765
Good were their words of greeting;
Each joyed in other's sight;
Great peril attends that meeting
Should Mary forget her knight.

For that high-born beauty so hemmed him about, 1770
Made so plain her meaning, the man must needs
Either take her tendered love or distastefully refuse.
His courtesy concerned him, lest crass he appear,
But more his soul's mischief, should he commit sin
And belie his loyal oath to the lord of that house. 1775
"God forbid!" said the bold knight, "That shall not befall!"
With a little fond laughter he lightly let pass
All the words of special weight that were sped his way;
"I find you much at fault," the fair one said,
"Who can be cold toward a creature so close by your side, 1780
Of all women in this world most wounded in heart,
Unless you have a sweetheart, one you hold dearer,
And allegiance to that lady so loyally knit
That you will never love another, as now I believe.
And, sir, if it be so, then say it, I beg you; 1785
By all your heart holds dear, hide it no longer
with guile."
"Lady, by Saint John,"
He answers with a smile,

"Lover have I none,   1790
        Nor will have, yet awhile."

"Those words," said the woman, "are the worst of all,
But I have had my answer, and hard do I find it!
Kiss me now kindly; I can but go hence
To lament my life long like a maid lovelorn."   1795
She inclines her head quickly and kisses the knight,
Then straightens with a sigh, and says as she stands,
"Now, dear, ere I depart, do me this pleasure:
Give me some little gift, your glove or the like,
That I may think on you, man, and mourn the less."   1800
"Now by heaven," said he, "I wish I had here
My most precious possession, to put it in your hands,
For your deeds, beyond doubt, have often deserved
A repayment far passing my power to bestow.
But a love-token, lady, were of little avail;   1805
It is not to your honor to have at this time
A glove as a guerdon from Gawain's hand,
And I am here on an errand in unknown realms
And have no bearers with baggage with becoming gifts,
Which distresses me, madame, for your dear sake.   1810
A man must keep within his compass: account it neither grief
                        nor slight."
                "Nay, noblest knight alive,"
                Said that beauty of body white,
                "Though you be loath to give,   1815
                Yet you shall take, by right."

She reached out a rich ring, wrought all of gold,
With a splendid stone displayed on the band
That flashed before his eyes like a fiery sun;
It was worth a king's wealth, you may well believe. 1820
But he waved it away with these ready words:
"Before God, good lady, I forego all gifts;
None have I to offer, nor any will I take."
And she urged it on him eagerly, and ever he refused,
And vowed in very earnest, prevail she would not.   1825
And she sad to find it so, and said to him then,
"If my ring is refused for its rich cost—
You would not be my debtor for so dear a thing—
I shall give you my girdle; you gain less thereby."
She released a knot lightly, and loosened a belt   1830
That was caught about her kirtle, the bright cloak beneath,
Of a gay green silk, with gold overwrought,
And the borders all bound with embroidery fine,
And this she presses upon him, and pleads with a smile,
Unworthy though it were, that it would not be scorned. 1835
But the man still maintains that he means to accept
Neither gold nor any gift, till by God's grace
The fate that lay before him was fully achieved.

"And be not offended, fair lady, I beg,
And give over your offer, for ever I must   1840
                    decline.
                    I am grateful for favor shown
                    Past all deserts of mine,
                    And ever shall be your own
                    True servant, rain or shine."   1845

"Now does my present displease you," she promptly inquired,
"Because it seems in your sight so simple a thing?
And belike, as it is little, it is less to praise,
But if the virtue that invests it were verily known,
It would be held, I hope, in higher esteem.   1850
For the man that possesses this piece of silk,
If he bore it on his body, belted about,
There is no hand under heaven that could hew him down,
For he could not be killed by any craft on earth."
Then the man began to muse, and mainly he thought   1855
It was a pearl for his plight, the peril to come
When he gains the Green Chapel to get his reward:
Could he escape unscathed, the scheme were noble!
Then he bore with her words and withstood them no more,
And she repeated her petition and pleaded anew,
And he granted it, and gladly she gave him the belt,   1860
And besought him for her sake to conceal it well,
Lest the noble lord should know—and the knight agrees
That not a soul save themselves shall see it thenceforth
                    with sight.   1865
                    He thanked her with fervent heart,
                    As often as ever he might;
                    Three times, before they part,
                    She has kissed the stalwart knight.

Then the lady took her leave, and left him there,   1870
For more mirth with that man she might not have.
When she was gone, Sir Gawain got from his bed,
Arose and arrayed him in his rich attire;
Tucked away the token the temptress had left,
Laid it reliably where he looked for it after.   1875
And then with good cheer to the chapel he goes,
Approached a priest in private, and prayed to be taught
To lead a better life and lift up his mind,
Lest he be among the lost when he must leave this world.
And shamefaced at shrift he showed his misdeeds   1880
From the largest to the least, and asked the Lord's mercy,
And called on his confessor to cleanse his soul,
And he absolved him of his sins as safe and as clean
As if the dread Day of Judgment should dawn on the morrow.
And then he made merry amid the fine ladies   1885
With deft-footed dances and dalliance light,

As never until now, while the afternoon wore
away.
He delighted all around him,
And all agreed, that day,
They never before had found him
So gracious and so gay.

Now peaceful be his pasture, and love play him fair!
The host is on horseback, hunting afield;
He has finished off this fox that he followed so long:
As he leapt a low hedge to look for the villain
Where he heard all the hounds in hot pursuit,
Reynard comes racing out of a rough thicket,
And all the rabble in a rush, right at his heels.
The man beholds the beast, and bides his time,
And bares his bright sword, and brings it down hard,
And he blenches from the blade, and backward he starts;
A hound hurries up and hinders that move,
And before the horse's feet they fell on him at once
And ripped the rascal's throat with a wrathful din.
The lord soon alighted and lifted him free,
Swiftly snatched him up from the snapping jaws,
Holds him over his head, halloos with a will,
And the dogs bayed the dirge, that had done him to death.
Hunters hastened thither with horns at their lips,
Sounding the assembly till they saw him at last.
When that comely company was come in together,
All that bore bugles blew them at once,
And the others all hallooed, that had no horns.
It was the merriest medley that ever a man heard,
The racket that they raised for Sir Reynard's soul
that died.
Their hounds they praised and fed,
Fondling their heads with pride,
And they took Reynard the Red
And stripped away his hide.

And then they headed homeward, for evening had come,
Blowing many a blast on their bugles bright.
The lord at long last alights at his house,
Finds fire on the hearth where the fair knight waits,
Sir Gawain the good, that was glad in heart.
With the ladies, that loved him, he lingered at ease;
He wore a rich robe of blue, that reached to the earth
And a surcoat lined softly with sumptuous furs;
A hood of the same hue hung on his shoulders;
With bands of bright ermine embellished were both.
He comes to meet the man amid all the folk,
And greets him good-humoredly, and gaily he says,
"I shall follow forthwith the form of our pledge
That we framed to good effect amid fresh-filled cups."

1890

1895

1900

1905

1910

1915

1920

1925

1930

1935

He clasps him accordingly and kisses him thrice,
As amiably and as earnestly as ever he could.
"By heaven," said the host, "you have had some luck
Since you took up this trade, if the terms were good."
"Never trouble about the terms," he returned at once,   1940
"Since all that I owe here is openly paid."
"Marry!" said the other man, "mine is much less,
For I have hunted all day, and nought have I got
But this foul fox pelt, the fiend take the goods!
Which but poorly repays those precious things   1945
That you have cordially conferred, those kisses three
                    so good."
                "Enough!" said Sir Gawain;
                "I thank you, by the rood!"
                And how the fox was slain   1950
                He told him, as they stood.

With minstrelsy and mirth, with all manner of meats,
They made as much merriment as any men might
(Amid laughing of ladies and light-hearted girls,
So gay grew Sir Gawain and the goodly host)   1955
Unless they had been besotted, or brainless fools.
The knight joined in jesting with that joyous folk,
Until at last it was late; ere long they must part,
And be off to their beds, as behooved them each one.
Then politely his leave of the lord of the house   1960
Our noble knight takes, and renews his thanks:
"The courtesies countless accorded me here,
Your kindness at this Christmas, may heaven's King repay!
Henceforth, if you will have me, I hold you my liege,
And so, as I have said, I must set forth tomorrow,   1965
If I may take some trusty man to teach, as you promised,
The way to the Green Chapel, that as God allows
I shall see my fate fulfilled on the first of the year."
"In good faith," said the good man, "with a good will
Every promise on my part shall be fully performed."   1970
He assigns him a servant to set him on the path,
To see him safe and sound over the snowy hills,
To follow the fastest way through forest green
                    and grove.
                Gawain thanks him again,   1975
                So kind his favors prove,
                And of the ladies then
                He takes his leave, with love.

Courteously he kissed them, with care in his heart,
And often wished them well, with warmest thanks,   1980
Which they for their part were prompt to repay.
They commend him to Christ with disconsolate sighs;
And then in that hall with the household he parts—
Each man that he met, he remembered to thank

For his deeds of devotion and diligent pains,   1985
And the trouble he had taken to tend to his needs;
And each one as woeful, that watched him depart,
As he had lived with him loyally all his life long.
By lads bearing lights he was led to his chamber
And blithely brought to his bed, to be at his rest.   1990
How soundly he slept, I presume not to say,
For there were matters of moment his thoughts might well
> pursue.
>> Let him lie and wait;
>> He has little more to do,   1995
>> Then listen, while I relate
>> How they kept their rendezvous.

Part IV

Now the New Year draws near, and the night passes,
The day dispels the dark, by the Lord's decree;
But wild weather awoke in the world without: 2000
The clouds in the cold sky cast down their snow
With great gusts from the north, grievous to bear.
Sleet showered aslant upon shivering beasts;
The wind warbled wild as it whipped from aloft,
And drove the drifts deep in the dales below.   2005
Long and well he listens, that lies in his bed;
Though he lifts not his eyelids, little he sleeps;
Each crow of the cock he counts without fail.
Readily from his rest he rose before dawn,
For a lamp had been left him, that lighted his chamber.   2010
He called to his chamberlain, who quickly appeared,
And bade him get him his gear, and gird his good steed,
And he sets about briskly to bring in his arms,
And makes ready his master in manner most fit.
First he clad him in his clothes, to keep out the cold,   2015
And then his other harness, made handsome anew,
His plate-armor of proof, polished with pains,
The rings of his rich mail rid of their rust,
And all was fresh as at first, and for this he gave thanks
> indeed.   2020
>> With pride he wears each piece,
>> New-furbished for his need:
>> No gayer from here to Greece;
>> He bids them bring his steed.

In his richest raiment he robed himself then: 2025
His crested coat-armor, close-stitched with craft,
With stones of strange virtue on silk velvet set;
All bound with embroidery on borders and seams
And lined warmly and well with furs of the best.
Yet he left not his love-gift, the lady's girdle;   2030

Gawain, for his own good, forgot not that:
When the bright sword was belted and bound on his haunches,
Then twice with that token he twined him about.
Sweetly did he swathe him in that swatch of silk,
That girdle of green so goodly to see,   2035
That against the gay red showed gorgeous bright.
Yet he wore not for its wealth that wondrous girdle,
Nor pride in its pendants, though polished they were,
Though glittering gold gleamed at the tips,
But to keep himself safe when consent he must   2040
To endure a deadly dint, and all defense
                         denied.
               And now the bold knight came
               Into the courtyard wide;
               That folk of worthy fame   2045
               He thanks on every side.

Then was Gringolet girt, that was great and huge,
And had sojourned safe and sound, and savored his fare;
He pawed the earth in his pride, that princely steed.
The good knight draws near him and notes well his look,   2050
And says sagely to himself, and soberly swears,
"Here is a household in hall that upholds the right!
The man that maintains it, may happiness be his!
Likewise the dear lady, may love betide her!
If thus they in charity cherish a guest   2055
That are honored here on earth, may they have His reward
That reigns high in heaven—and also you all;
And were I to live in this land but a little while,
I should willingly reward you, and well, if I might."
Then he steps into the stirrup and bestrides his mount;   2060
His shield is shown forth; on his shoulder he casts it;
Strikes the side of his steed with his steel spurs,
And he starts across the stones, nor stands any longer
                         to prance.
               On horseback was the swain   2065
               That bore his spear and lance;
               "May Christ this house maintain
               And guard it from mischance!"

The bridge was brought down, and the broad gates
Unbarred and carried back upon both sides;   2070
He commended him to Christ, and crossed over the planks;
Praised the noble porter, who prayed on his knees
That God save Sir Gawain, and bade him good day,
And went on his way alone with the man
That was to lead him ere long to that luckless place   2075
Where the dolorous dint must be dealt him at last.
Under bare boughs they ride, where steep banks rise,
Over high cliffs they climb, where cold snow clings;
The heavens held aloof, but heavy thereunder
Mist mantled the moors, moved on the slopes.   2080

Each hill had a hat, a huge cape of cloud;
Brooks bubbled and broke over broken rocks,
Flashing in freshets that waterfalls fed.
Roundabout was the road that ran through the wood
Till the sun at that season was soon to rise,⁣ 2085
    that day.
    They were on a hilltop high;
    The white snow round them lay;
    The man that rode nearby
    Now bade his master stay.⁣ 2090

"For I have seen you here safe at the set time,
And now you are not far from that notable place
That you have sought for so long with such special pains.
But this I say for certain, since I know you, sir knight,
And have your good at heart, and hold you dear—⁣ 2095
Would you heed well my words, it were worth your while—
You are rushing into risks that you reck not of:
There is a villain in yon valley, the veriest on earth,
For he is rugged and rude, and ready with his fists,
And most immense in his mold of mortals alive,⁣ 2100
And his body bigger than the best four
That are in Arthur's house, Hector or any.
He gets his grim way at the Green Chapel;
None passes by that place so proud in his arms
That he does not dash him down with his deadly blows,⁣ 2105
For he is heartless wholly, and heedless of right,
For be it chaplain or churl that by the Chapel rides,
Monk or mass-priest or any man else,
He would as soon strike him dead as stand on two feet.
Wherefore I say, just as certain as you sit there astride,⁣ 2110
You cannot but be killed, if his counsel holds,
For he would trounce you in a trice, had you twenty lives
    for sale.
    He has lived long in this land
    And dealt out deadly bale;⁣ 2115
    Against his heavy hand
    Your power cannot prevail.

"And so, good Sir Gawain, let the grim man be;
Go off by some other road, in God's own name!
Leave by some other land, for the love of Christ,⁣ 2120
And I shall get me home again, and give you my word
That I shall swear by God's self and the saints above,
By heaven and by my halidom and other oaths more,
To conceal this day's deed, nor say to a soul
That ever you fled for fear from any that I knew."⁣ 2125
"Many thanks!" said the other man—and demurring he speaks—
"Fair fortune befall you for your friendly words!
And conceal this day's deed I doubt not you would,
But though you never told the tale, if I turned back now,

Forsook this place for fear, and fled, as you say,   2130
I were a caitiff coward; I could not be excused.
But I must to the Chapel to chance my luck
And say to that same man such words as I please,
Befall what may befall through Fortune's will
               or whim.   2135
        Though he be a quarrelsome knave
        With a cudgel great and grim,
        The Lord is strong to save:
        His servants trust in Him."

"Marry," said the man, "since you tell me so much,   2140
And I see you are set to seek your own harm,
If you crave a quick death, let me keep you no longer!
Put your helm on your head, your hand on your lance,
And ride the narrow road down yon rocky slope
Till it brings you to the bottom of the broad valley.   2145
Then look a little ahead, on your left hand,
And you will soon see before you that self-same Chapel,
And the man of great might that is master there.
Now goodbye in God's name, Gawain the noble!
For all the world's wealth I would not stay here,   2150
Or go with you in this wood one footstep further!"
He tarried no more to talk, but turned his bridle,
Hit his horse with his heels as hard as he might,
Leaves the knight alone, and off like the wind
               goes leaping.   2155
        "By God," said Gawain then,
        "I shall not give way to weeping;
        God's will be done, amen!
        I commend me to His keeping."

He puts his heels to his horse, and picks up the path;   2160
Goes in beside a grove where the ground is steep,
Rides down the rough slope right to the valley;
And then he looked a little about him—the landscape was wild,
And not a soul to be seen, nor sign of a dwelling,
But high banks on either hand hemmed it about,   2165
With many a ragged rock and rough-hewn crag;
The skies seemed scored by the scowling peaks.
Then he halted his horse, and hoved there a space,
And sought on every side for a sight of the Chapel,
But no such place appeared, which puzzled him sore,   2170
Yet he saw some way off what seemed like a mound,
A hillock high and broad, hard by the water,
Where the stream fell in foam down the face of the steep
And bubbled as if it boiled on its bed below.
The knight urges his horse, and heads for the knoll;   2175
Leaps lightly to earth; loops well the rein
Of his steed to a stout branch, and stations him there.
He strides straight to the mound, and strolls all about,

Much wondering what it was, but no whit the wiser;
It had a hole at one end, and on either side,   2180
And was covered with coarse grass in clumps all without,
And hollow all within, like some old cave,
Or a crevice of an old crag—he could not discern
                aright.
        "Can this be the Chapel Green?   2185
        Alack!" said the man, "Here might
        The devil himself be seen
        Saying matins at black midnight!"

"Now by heaven," said he, "it is bleak hereabouts;
This prayer-house is hideous, half-covered with grass!   2190
Well may the grim man mantled in green
Hold here his orisons, in hell's own style!
Now I feel it is the Fiend, in my five wits,
That has tempted me to this tryst, to take my life;
This is a Chapel of mischance, may the mischief take it!   2195
As accursed a country church as I came upon ever!"
With his helm on his head, his lance in his hand,
He stalks toward the steep wall of that strange house.
Then he heard, on the hill, behind a hard rock,
Beyond the brook, from the bank, a most barbarous din: 2200
Lord! it clattered in the cliff fit to cleave it in two,
As one upon a grindstone ground a great scythe!
Lord! it whirred like a mill-wheel whirling about!
Lord! it echoed loud and long, lamentable to hear!
Then "By heaven," said the bold knight, "That business up there   2205
Is arranged for my arrival, or else I am much
                misled.
        Let God work! Ah me!
        All hope of help has fled!
        Forfeit my life may be   2210
        But noise I do not dread."

Then he listened no longer, but loudly he called,
"Who has power in this place, high parley to hold?
For none greets Sir Gawain, or gives him good day;
If any would a word with him, let him walk forth   2215
And speak now or never, to speed his affairs."
"Abide," said one on the bank above over his head,
"And what I promised you once shall straightway be given."
Yet he stayed not his grindstone, nor stinted its noise,
But worked awhile at his whetting before he would rest,   2220
And then he comes around a crag, from a cave in the rocks,
Hurtling out of hiding with a hateful weapon,
A Danish ax devised for that day's deed,
With a broad blade and bright, bent in a curve,
Filed to a fine edge—four feet it measured   2225
By the length of the lace that was looped round the haft.
And in form as at first, the fellow all green,

His lordly face and his legs, his locks and his beard,
Save that firm upon two feet forward he strides,
Sets a hand on the ax-head, the haft to the earth; 2230
When he came to the cold stream, and cared not to wade,
He vaults over on his ax, and advances amain
On a broad bank of snow, overbearing and brisk
     of mood.
    Little did the knight incline 2235
    When face to face they stood;
    Said the other man, "Friend mine,
    It seems your word holds good!"

"God love you, Sir Gawain!" said the Green Knight then,
"And well met this morning, man, at my place! 2240
And you have followed me faithfully and found me betimes,
And on the business between us we both are agreed:
Twelve months ago today you took what was yours,
And you at this New Year must yield me the same.
And we have met in these mountains, remote from all eyes: 2245
There is none here to halt us or hinder our sport;
Unhasp your high helm, and have here your wages;
Make no more demur than I did myself
When you hacked off my head with one hard blow."
"No, by God," said Sir Gawain, "that granted me life, 2250
I shall grudge not the guerdon, grim though it prove;
Bestow but one stroke, and I shall stand still,
And you may lay on as you like till the last of my part
     be paid.
    He proffered, with good grace, 2255
    His bare neck to the blade,
    And feigned a cheerful face:
    He scorned to seem afraid.

Then the grim man in green gathers his strength,
Heaves high the heavy ax to hit him the blow. 2260
With all the force in his frame he fetches it aloft,
With a grimace as grim as he would grind him to bits;
Had the blow he bestowed been as big as he threatened,
A good knight and gallant had gone to his grave.
But Gawain at the great ax glanced up aside 2265
As down it descended with death-dealing force,
And his shoulders shrank a little from the sharp iron.
Abruptly the brawny man breaks off the stroke,
And then reproved with proud words that prince among knights.
"You are not Gawain the glorious," the green man said, 2270
"That never fell back on field in the face of the foe,
And now you flee for fear, and have felt no harm:
Such news of that knight I never heard yet!
I moved not a muscle when you made to strike,
Nor caviled at the cut in King Arthur's house; 2275
My head fell to my feet, yet steadfast I stood,

And you, all unharmed, are wholly dismayed—
Wherefore the better man I, by all odds,
                    must be."
                    Said Gawain, "Strike once more;   2280
                    I shall neither flinch nor flee;
                    But if my head falls to the floor
                    There is no mending me!"

"But go on, man, in God's name, and get to the point!
Deliver me my destiny, and do it out of hand,   2285
For I shall stand to the stroke and stir not an inch
Till your ax has hit home—on my honor I swear it!"
"Have at thee then!" said the other, and heaves it aloft,
And glares down as grimly as he had gone mad.
He made a mighty feint, but marred not his hide;   2290
Withdrew the ax adroitly before it did damage.
Gawain gave no ground, nor glanced up aside,
But stood still as a stone, or else a stout stump
That is held in hard earth by a hundred roots.
Then merrily does he mock him, the man all in green: 2295
"So now you have your nerve again, I needs must strike;
Uphold the high knighthood that Arthur bestowed,
And keep your neck-bone clear, if this cut allows!"
Then was Gawain gripped with rage, and grimly he said,
"Why, thrash away, tyrant, I tire of your threats;   2300
You make such a scene, you must frighten yourself.
Said the green fellow, "In faith, so fiercely you speak
That I shall finish this affair, nor further grace
                    allow."
                    He stands prepared to strike   2305
                    And scowls with both lip and brow;
                    No marvel if the man mislike
                    Who can hope no rescue now.

He gathered up the grim ax and guided it well:
Let the barb at the blade's end brush the bare throat;   2310
He hammered down hard, yet harmed him no whit
Save a scratch on one side, that severed the skin;
The end of the hooked edge entered the flesh,
And a little blood lightly leapt to the earth.
And when the man beheld his own blood bright on the snow,   2315
He sprang a spear's length with feet spread wide,
Seized his high helm, and set it on his head,
Shoved before his shoulders the shield at his back,
Bares his trusty blade, and boldly he speaks—
Not since he was a babe born of his mother   2320
Was he once in this world one-half so blithe—
"Have done with your hacking—harry me no more!
I have borne, as behooved, one blow in this place;
If you make another move I shall meet it midway

And promptly, I promise you, pay back each blow 2325
                    with brand.
                    One stroke acquits me here;
                    So did our covenant stand
                    In Arthur's court last year—
                    Wherefore, sir, hold your hand!" 2330

He lowers the long ax and leans on it there,
Sets his arms on the head, the haft on the earth,
And beholds the bold knight that bides there afoot,
How he faces him fearless, fierce in full arms,
And plies him with proud words—it pleases him well. 2335
Then once again gaily to Gawain he calls,
And in a loud voice and lusty, delivers these words:
"Bold fellow, on this field your anger forbear!
No man has made demands here in manner uncouth,
Nor done, save as duly determined at court. 2340
I owed you a hit and you have it; be happy therewith!
The rest of my rights here I freely resign.
Had I been a bit busier, a buffet, perhaps,
I could have dealt more directly, and done you some harm.
First I flourished with a feint, in frolicsome mood, 2345
And left your hide unhurt—and here I did well
By the fair terms we fixed on the first night;
And fully and faithfully you followed accord:
Gave over all your gains as a good man should.
A second feint, sir, I assigned for the morning 2350
You kissed my comely wife—each kiss you restored.
For both of these there behooved but two feigned blows
                    by right.
                    True men pay what they owe;
                    No danger then in sight. 2355
                    You failed at the third throw,
                    So take my tap, sir knight.

"For that is my belt about you, that same braided girdle,
My wife it was that wore it; I know well the tale,
And the count of your kisses and your conduct too, 2360
And the wooing of my wife—it was all my scheme!
She made trial of a man most faultless by far
Of all that ever walked over the wide earth;
As pearls to white peas, more precious and prized,
So is Gawain, in good faith, to other gay knights. 2365
Yet you lacked, sir, a little in loyalty there,
But the cause was not cunning, nor courtship either,
But that you loved your own life; the less, then, to blame."
The other stout knight in a study stood a long while,
So gripped with grim rage that his great heart shook. 2370
All the blood of his body burned in his face
As he shrank back in shame from the man's sharp speech.
The first words that fell from the fair knight's lips:

"Accursed be a cowardly and covetous heart!
In you is villainy and vice, and virtue laid low!"   2375
Then he grasps the green girdle and lets go the knot,
Hands it over in haste, and hotly he says:
"Behold there my falsehood, ill hap betide it!
Your cut taught me cowardice, care for my life,
And coveting came after, contrary both   2380
To largesse and loyalty belonging to knights.
Now am I faulty and false, that fearful was ever
Of disloyalty and lies, bad luck to them both!
      and greed.
    I confess, knight, in this place,   2385
    Most dire is my misdeed;
    Let me gain back your good grace,
    And thereafter I shall take heed."

Then the other laughed aloud, and lightly he said,
"Such harm as I have had, I hold it quite healed.   2390
You are so fully confessed, your failings made known,
And bear the plain penance of the point of my blade,
I hold you polished as a pearl, as pure and as bright
As you had lived free of fault since first you were born.
And I give you, sir, this girdle that is gold-hemmed   2395
And green as my garments, that, Gawain, you may
Be mindful of this meeting when you mingle in throng
With nobles of renown—and known by this token
How it chanced at the Green Chapel, to chivalrous knights.
And you shall in this New Year come yet again   2400
And we shall finish out our feast in my fair hall,
      with cheer."
    He urged the knight to stay,
    And said, "With my wife so dear
    We shall see you friends this day,   2405
    Whose enmity touched you near."

"Indeed," said the doughty knight, and doffed his high helm,
And held it in his hands as he offered his thanks,
"I have lingered long enough—may good luck be yours,
And He reward you well that all worship bestows!   2410
And commend me to that comely one, your courteous wife,
Both herself and that other, my honoured ladies,
That have trapped their true knight in their trammels so quaint.
But if a dullard should dote, deem it no wonder,
And through the wiles of a woman be wooed into sorrow,   2415
For so was Adam by one, when the world began,
And Solomon by many more, and Samson the mighty—
Delilah was his doom, and David thereafter
Was beguiled by Bathsheba, and bore much distress;
Now these were vexed by their devices—'twere a very joy   2420
Could one but learn to love, and believe them not.
For these were proud princes, most prosperous of old,

Past all lovers lucky, that languished under heaven,
       bemused.
    And one and all fell prey   2425
    To women that they had used;
    If I be led astray,
    Methinks I may be excused.

"But your girdle, God love you! I gladly shall take
And be pleased to possess, not for the pure gold,   2430
Nor the bright belt itself, nor the beauteous pendants,
Nor for wealth, nor worldly state, nor workmanship fine,
But a sign of excess it shall seem oftentimes
When I ride in renown, and remember with shame
The faults and the frailty of the flesh perverse,   2435
How its tenderness entices the foul taint of sin;
And so when praise and high prowess have pleased my heart,
A look at this love-lace will lower my pride.
But one thing would I learn, if you were not loath,
Since you are lord of yonder land where I have long sojourned 2440
With honor in your house—may you have His reward
That upholds all the heavens, highest on throne!
How runs your right name?—and let the rest go."
"That shall I give you gladly," said the Green Knight then;
"Bercilak de Hautdesert this barony I hold,   2445
Through the might of Morgan le Fay, that lodges at my house,
By subtleties of science and sorcerers' arts,
The mistress of Merlin, she has caught many a man,
For sweet love in secret she shared sometime
With that wizard, that knows well each one of your knights 2450
      and you.
    Morgan the Goddess, she,
    So styled by title true;
    None holds so high degree
    That her arts cannot subdue.   2455

"She guided me in this guise to your glorious hall,
To assay, if such it were, the surfeit of pride
That is rumored of the retinue of the Round Table.
She put this shape upon me to puzzle your wits,
To afflict the fair queen, and frighten her to death 2460
With awe of that elvish man that eerily spoke
With his head in his hand before the high table.
She was with my wife at home, that old withered lady,
Your own aunt is she, Arthur's half-sister,
The Duchess' daughter of Tintagel, that dear King Uther 2465
Got Arthur on after, that honored is now.
And therefore, good friend, come feast with your aunt;
Make merry in my house; my men hold you dear,
And I wish you as well, sir, with all my heart,
As any mortal man, for your matchless faith."   2470
But the knight said him nay, that he might by no means.

They clasped then and kissed, and commended each other
To the Prince of Paradise, and parted with one
        assent.
      Gawain sets out anew;   2475
      Toward the court his course is bent;
      And the knight all green in hue,
      Wheresoever he wished, he went.

Wild ways in the world our worthy knight rides
On Gringolet, that by grace had been granted his life. 2480
He harbored often in houses, and often abroad,
And with many valiant adventures verily he met
That I shall not take time to tell in this story.
The hurt was whole that he had had in his neck,
And the bright green belt on his body he bore,   2485
Oblique, like a baldric, bound at his side,
Below his left shoulder, laced in a knot,
In betokening of the blame he had borne for his fault;
And so to court in due course he comes safe and sound.
Bliss abounded in hall when the high-born heard 2490
That good Gawain was come; glad tidings they thought it.
The king kisses the knight, and the queen as well,
And many a comrade came to clasp him in arms,
And eagerly they asked, and awesomely he told,
Confessed all his cares and discomfitures many, 2495
How it chanced at the Chapel, what cheer made the knight,
The love of the lady, the green lace at last.
The nick on his neck he naked displayed
That he got in his disgrace at the Green Knight's hands,
        alone.   2500
      With rage in heart he speaks,
      And grieves with many a groan;
      The blood burns in his cheeks
      For shame at what must be shown.

"Behold, sir," said he, and handles the belt,   2505
"This is the blazon of the blemish that I bear on my neck;
This is the sign of sore loss that I have suffered there
For the cowardice and coveting that I came to there;
This is the badge of false faith that I was found in there,
And I must bear it on my body till I breathe my last. 2510
For one may keep a deed dark, but undo it no whit,
For where a fault is made fast, it is fixed evermore."
The king comforts the knight, and the court all together
Agree with gay laughter and gracious intent
That the lords and the ladies belonging to the Table, 2515
Each brother of that band, a baldric should have,
A belt borne oblique, of a bright green,
To be worn with one accord for that worthy's sake.
So that was taken as a token by the Table Round,
And he honored that had it, evermore after,   2520

As the best book of knighthood bids it be known.
In the old days of Arthur this happening befell;
The books of Brutus' deeds bear witness thereto
Since Brutus, the bold knight, embarked for this land
After the siege ceased at Troy and the city fared   2525
                    amiss.
            Many such, ere we were born,
            Have befallen here, ere this.
            May He that was crowned with thorn
            Bring all men to His bliss! Amen.   2530

The Metrical Form

The "alliterative long line" in which *Sir Gawain and the Green Knight* is composed may best be described as having a basic form with numerous variations. In this basic form, the line is divided by its phrasing into two half-lines, each of which contains two clearly predominant stresses or "chief syllables." There are thus four chief syllables to a line; of these, the first three are linked by alliteration, beginning with the same letter or occasionally with a combination of letters such as *sp* or *st*. If capital C's are placed above the line to mark chief syllables and a's and x's below the line to mark alliteration or its absence, with a slant-bar to divide the half-lines, the metrical patterns of two lines of the basic type may be indicated thus:

<pre>
            C   C   C   C
With all the meat and the mirth that men could devise,
          a   a   /   a   x

      C   C   C   C
Such gaiety and glee, glorious to hear   (45-46)
      a   a   /a   x
</pre>

(In these and other examples, the wording of the translation is close enough to that of the original so that there is no significant difference in metrical pattern between the two.) Something of the variety possible within the basic form may be shown by another pair of lines:

<pre>
         C   C   C   C
With many birds unblithe upon bare twigs
         a   a   /   a   x

      C   C   C   C
That peeped most piteously for pain of the cold.   (746-47)
      a   a   /   a   x
</pre>

In the first of these, the two stresses of the second half-line occur side by side; in the next, the second stress is separated from the third by three un-stressed syllables. The alliterative long line is much more flexible in its feet or "measures" than the classic iambic pentameter line of English verse from Spenser through Frost.

I have spoken of four "clearly predominant" stresses as constituting the basic form of the line. There are many lines, however, which contain stressed syllables above and beyond the basic four, and the scansion of some of the heaviest of these lines has been subject to dispute. Consider, for example, the sequence

> When he had on his arms, his harness was rich,
> The least latchet or loop laden with gold.   (590-91)

The first has the basic form; it also happens to illustrate the possibility, optional for the poet, of combining words beginning with a vowel with words beginning with *h* in the alliterative pattern. But in the second there are five "stressed" syllables, four of which alliterate. This so called "extended form" is a distinctive feature of the alliterative verse of the *Gawain* poet. I contend that in all such lines, four syllables can be seen as having major importance, falling at rhythmically equivalent intervals in the "swing" of the line-sequence. In this example, *least* and *loop* may be distinguished as "major chief syllables" (C's), and *latchet* may be called a "minor chief syllable" (c). The rhythm of "least latchet or loop" is very much like that of "pease porridge hot" in the nursery rhyme; in neither does minor rank imply an unnatural reduction of stress. The metrical pattern of the line may be indicated as follows:

<pre>
      C   c   C   C   C
The least latchet or loop laden with gold.
      a   a   a /a   x
</pre>

According to the above interpretation, the triply-alliterating "heavy" half-lines which occur frequently in some parts of the poem and sporadically throughout are seen as stretching rather than breaking the basic structure of two *major* stresses per half-line; of the three heavy syllables they contain, one will always be given minor rank. This principle cannot, of course, be demonstrated by lines taken out of context; what is crucial is the rhythm of the verse, the basic momentum which establishes itself cumulatively and is instinctively felt. The modern student should have no difficulty in reading the translation aloud or to himself, provided he realizes that the relation between stress and alliteration is very flexible indeed (as also in the original): nonalliterating syllables may receive major stress, while alliterating syllables may receive minor stress or none at all. Some of the variations in form resulting from these possibilities are described in the following section.

VARIANT FORMS

In many half-lines of the extended type, only two of the three stressed syllables alliterate, and these two may or may not have major rank:

<pre>
      C   C   c   C   c C
And Gawain the good knight in gay bed lies   (1179)
      a   a   x   / a   x x

      C   c   C   C   C
The blood for sheer shame shot to his face   (317)
      x   a   a   /a   x

    C c   C   C   C
The old ancient lady, highest she sits   (1001)
    a a   x   /a   x

       C   c   C   C   C
With good couters and gay, and gloves of plate   (583)
       a   x   a   /   a   x
</pre>

The relation of adjective to noun in "good knight" and "gay bed," above, is comparable to that in "Baa, baa, black sheep" or "Taffy came to my house." These similarities in metrical pattern between *Gawain* and nursery rhymes are not accidental; both kinds of verse are traditional, and, what is more important, both are associated importantly with reading aloud or recitation. The equally important difference between the two is that the rhythm of the nursery rhyme is uniform; major and minor stresses occur in regular alternation, and there may be distortion of natural stressing, as when we read "Pease porridge *in* the pot." In *Gawain*, stresses of minor rank constitute variation, not the norm, and the metrical patterns of the long lines are thoroughly consistent with the stress patterns of the spoken language.

Another sort of variation found in the long lines of *Gawain* is the placement of the alliteration on unstressed syllables such as prefixes, prepositions, and auxiliary verbs:

```
        C           C    C          C
"Dear dame, on this day dismay you no whit"     (470)
(a)     a           a   /a          x
```

```
          C      C         C      C
"And that is best, I believe, and behooves me now"     (1216)
          a      a    /    a         x
```

(In the above example, alliteration falls on the preposition *by* in the original; see the first scanned passage below.)

```
          C    c  C       C              C
For I have hunted all day, and nought have I got     (1943)
          a    a  x  /    x        a     x
```

(Here I have marked only the alliterating syllables essential to the form.)

A few other variant alliterative patterns will be found both in the original and in the translation; I have tried not to make use of them more frequently than the poet himself did. The first half-line may contain only one alliterating syllable:

```
        C        C       C        C
The stranger before him stood there erect     (332)
        a        x      /a        x
```

In some lines, two alliterating combinations are present:

```
          C        C           C        C
And with undaunted countenance drew down his coat     (335)
          a        b          /a  (a)    b
```

Finally, there may be alliteration on all major stresses:

```
     C          C       C   c  C
Sir Bors and Sir Bedivere, big men both     (554)
     a          a      /a   x  a
```

The one hard and fast requirement of the form is the presence of an alliterative link between the two half-lines, even if the only alliterating syllable in the second half-line is unstressed. Lines in which such a link is entirely lacking have presumably been miscopied at some stage in the trans-mission of the text. In some cases it is impossible to be sure how the orig-inal must have read, but in others the solution is clear, as when *milk-white*, in a second half-line (958) otherwise lacking alliteration, is emended to alliterating *chalk-white*, a word used elsewhere by the poet.

As the above discussion makes obvious, here is God's plenty. The chief danger for the translator, I think, is not that he may fail to satisfy the re-quirements of the verse, but that he may elaborate too much. Any prac-tising poet knows that it is easier to turn on the alliteration than to turn it off, and though the *Gawain* poet liked to make repetitive use of sounds, he did not allow this penchant to dominate his art. The same point may be made with regard to the extended forms: the translator must not load his lines to the point where the underlying rhythm of four major chief syllables is obscured. It is the basic form to which the verse must continu-ally return and against which the heavier and more ornate forms must be measured.

In saying earlier that examples quoted from the translation did not differ significantly in their metrical patterns from the original lines, I was taking for granted certain conclusions as to the poet's language. I have no doubt of the validity of these conclusions, and have argued for them in detail elsewhere. It is my view that the speech of the *Gawain* poet's time and place had evolved in the direction of modern English to the point where the final -*e* familiar to the student of Chaucer's verse was no longer pro-nounced. This -*e* was used by the *Gawain* poet as an archaism in a few of the rhymed lines of the "wheels," described below, but was never used in the alliterative long line. To be specific, in the example "With many birds unblithe upon bare twigs," cited above, the word *bare* would, I believe, have been a monosyllable in the original just as it is today. This fact has the very important consequence of making possible not merely the ap-proximation, but the reproduction of the metrical patterns of *Gawain* in a modern translation (not, of course, line for line, but in the poem as a whole). "Ther watz mete, ther watz myrthe, ther watz much joye" (1007) is reproduced by the modern English translation "There was meat, there was mirth, there was much joy" not only in wording but in metrical pattern, despite the final -*e*'s of the original spelling.

THE RHYMED LINES

Gawain, like certain other poems composed late in its tradition, com-bines alliterative with rhymed verse. Paragraphs of long alliterative lines of varying length are followed by a single line of two syllables, called the bob, and a group of four three-stressed lines called the wheel. These five lines rhyme as in the following example:

<pre>
            C   c   C   C   C
On many broad hills and high Britain he sets,
         a   (b)   (b) /a   (b) x
                    C
                most fair.
</pre>

<pre>
        C   C   C
Where war and wrack and wonder
      C   C   C
By shifts have sojourned there,
        C   C   C
And bliss by turns with blunder
        C   C   C
In that land's lot had share.   (14–19)
</pre>

The metrical patterns of the rhyming lines are easy to recognize, closely resembling those of modern iambic verse.

SPECIMEN SCANSIONS

I have chosen for detailed metrical analysis two passages illustrating different kinds of metrical effect, presenting these both in the original and translation. The first, taken from the description of the castle to which Gawain comes on his journey, contains a number of extended lines; such "clusters" occur elsewhere in passages of detailed description. The second, taken from the conversation of the first bedchamber scene, contains a number of lines in which alliteration falls on unstressed syllables; the poet seems inclined to use lines of this sort in quoted speeches, especially those of the lady. In the transcriptions of Middle English passages, *u* has been substituted for *v* and *v* for *u* in accordance with modern practice; *th* for the Middle English letter *thorn*; *y* for Middle English *yogh* at the beginnings of words, *gh* in medial position, and *z* in final position. A single emendation, *gay* for nonalliterating *fair* in line 1208, is standard in modern editions of the poem.

1. Lines 785–93

<pre>
    C   c   C   C   C
The burne bode on bonk, that on blonk hoved,
    a   a   a   /   a   x

      C   c   C   C   C
Of the depe double dich that drof to the place;
      a   a   a   /   a   x

    C   c   C   C   C
The walle wod in the water wonderly depe,
    a   a   a   /a   x

    C   C   c   C   C
And eft a ful huge heght hit haled up on lofte,
    a   a   a   /   a   x

    C   c   C C   C
Of harde hewen ston up to the tablez,
    a   a   x /a   x
</pre>

```
       C                  C                C  C
Enbaned under the abataylment in the best lawe;
       a                  a             /     a  x

             C          C  C           C
And sythen garytez ful gaye gered bitwene,
             a          a   /a         x

            C        C          C          C
Wyth mony luflych loupe that louked ful clene:
            a        a      /      a        x

   c    C            C    C            C
A better barbican that burne blusched upon never.
   a    a            a   /a           x
```

```
         C          C       C           C
The man on his mount remained on the bank
         a          a    /  a           x

          C   c     C           C           C
Of the deep double moat that defended the place.
          a   a     x   /       a           x

         C   c        C    C         C
The wall went in the water wondrous deep,
         a   a        a   /a         x

          C   c  C   C           C
And a long way aloft it loomed overhead.
          a   x  a   /a          x

          C      c   C           C           C
It was built of stone blocks to the battlements' height,
          a      x   a   /       a           x

        C           C         C          C
With corbels under cornices in comeliest style;
        a           a      /  a          x

   C   c     C        C         C
Watch-towers trusty protected the gate,
   x   a     a     /  a         x

            C     c  C         C           C
With many a lean loophole, to look from within:
            x     a  a     /   a           x

   C    c   C           C        c   C
A better-made barbican the knight beheld never.
   a    x   a        /   b        a   b
```

2. Lines 1208–17

```
      C           C                 C  C
"God moroun, Sir Gawayn," sayde that gay lady,
  a           a         /        a   x

          C       C                C   C
"Ye ar a sleper unslyghe, that mon may slyde hider;
          a       a       /            a   x

        C   C      C            C
Now ar ye tan astyt! Bot true uus may schape,
        a   a  /  a          x

      C                 C    C  c   C
I schal bynde yow in your bedde, that be ye trayst!"
      a                 a    /x   a   x

    C         C  C        C
Al laghande the lady lanced tho bourdez.
  a         a  /a       x

        C    C         C          C
"Goud moroun, gay," quoth Gawayn the blythe,
  a         a      /     a         x

          C            C         C     c C
"Me schal worthe at your wille, and that me wel lykez,
          a            a     /   x       a  x

    C      C          C          C
For I yelde me yederly, and yeghe after grace,
    a      a         /    a          x

            C        C            C    C
And that is the best, be my dome, for me byhovez nede!"
          a    a    x   /        a       x

            C       C          C    c  C
And thus he bourded ayayn with mony a blythe laghter.
          a       x  /    x       a       x
```

```
      C           C              C  C
"Good morning, Sir Gawain," said that gay lady,
  a               a       /       a   x

    C   c      C      C         C
"A slack sleeper you are, to let one slip in!
  a   a        x  /  x       a   x
```

       C   C   C   C
Now you are taken in a trice — a truce we must make,
       a   a   / a   x

       C   C   C   C
Or I shall bind you in your bed, of that be assured."
        a   a / x   a   x

    C   C   C C
Thus laughing lightly that lady jested.
    a   a   /   a x

      C   C   C   C
"Good morning, good lady," said Gawain the blithe,
a   a   / a   x

     C   C   C   C
"Be it with me as you will; I am well content!
   a   a /   a   x

     C   C   C   C
For I surrender myself, and sue for your grace,
  a   a / a   x

       C C   C   C
And that is best, I believe, and behooves me now."
        a   a   / a   x

  C   C   C   C
Thus jested in answer that gentle knight.
  a   x   /   a   x

Reading Suggestions

Sir Gawain and the Green Knight, ed. J. R. R. Tolkien and E. V. Gordon. Oxford University Press. (Scholarly edition of the original text.)

PEARL *and* SIR GAWAIN AND THE GREEN KNIGHT, ed. A. C. Cawley. Everyman's Library, 346. (Original texts.)

Benson, Larry D. *Art and Tradition in* SIR GAWAIN AND THE GREEN KNIGHT. Rutgers University Press, 1965.

Borroff, Marie. SIR GAWAIN AND THE GREEN KNIGHT: *A Stylistic and Metrical Study.* Yale University Press, 1962.

Burrow, John A. A *Reading of* SIR GAWAIN AND THE GREEN KNIGHT. Barnes and Noble, 1966.